ISLAMO-COMMUNISM
The Communist Connection to Islamic Terrorism
By Chuck Morse

I0425569

Introduction,

Communism and Monotheism

The Communist Takeover of the Ottoman Empire

Communism and Iran

The Islamo-Communist war against Israel

Islam and the Soviet Union

Communism and Arab and Islamic states

Conclusion

This book is dedicated to Muslims who are suffering under the brutal steel-tipped jackboot of left-wing Islamo-Communism.

Introduction

Americans woke up to the threat of Islamic terror when Iranian students seized the American Embassy in Tehran in 1979 holding 52 hostages for over a year. The threat turned into a nightmare on September 11, 2001 with the attack by Islamic terrorists of the World Trade Center and the Pentagon. Since then al-Qaeda has launched terror attacks against innocents around the world. This book questions the conventional view that this is a war between radical Islam and the West. The contention presented here is that the enemy confronting the western democracies today is not Islam per se, nor is it even radical Islam, which could be viewed as the symptom of the disease.

The argument made here is that the real enemy confronting the free world is Communism cloaked in the garments of Islam. The same enemy that subverted Europe, starting with the French Revolutionary era Reign of Terror and reaching its apex of power with the two socialist European experiments of the 20th Century, Nazism and Communism, took root in the Islamic world and transformed Islam. Philosophically, Communism subverted monotheistic Islam and the Islamic Communists have thus made common cause with anti-Western elements around the world. Literally, Soviet Communism, assuming the mantle of terrorism and subversion from Nazism in 1945, after the defeat of Hitler, armed, trained, and financed Communist terrorist organizations in Islamic nations. The influence and the infrastructure of Soviet Communism continue today even though Communism is "dead" in the Soviet Union.

Karl Marx wrote in the introduction to The Communist Manifesto published in 1848: "A Spector is haunting Europe, the Spector of Communism." That same Spector, which bore fruit in Europe, haunts the Islamic world today. The Spector was imported into Islamic countries from Europe starting in the 19th Century and the transfer was enhanced with the 1917 Bolshevik Coup which became fully enthroned with the help of the Soviet Union. The Spector of Communism is disguised as Islam and, as such, Islamic Communism discredits one of the world's great monotheistic faiths. Islamo-Communism set the stage for Islamo-Communist terrorism and the war against both the West and moderate Islam.

Much has been written in the aftermath of 9/11 about Islam, its world conquering dogma called Jihad, its treatment of non-Muslims living in Muslim lands as Dhimmi or second class citizens, its abuse of women, its oppressive Sharia laws and its historic enslavement of Africa and all of these horrors are aspects of Islamic history and aspects of its present reality. Yet, there has been and remains a genuinely enlightened and peaceful tradition within Islam, a faith that has much in common with the monotheistic traditions of Judaism and Christianity. Modern radical fundamentalist Islam claims to reject western secular culture and ideologies yet the most radical Islamic states of today have a lot more in common with western inspired secular Communist countries such as the Soviet Union of Stalin, the China of Mao tse Tung or the Cambodia of Pol Pot than they have with traditional Islamic societies going back to the days of the prophet Mohammad.

There is nothing in Islam that would prohibit the development of such universal themes as civil rights, rights for women, private property, the free market, and other conventions that are inaccurately associated exclusively with secularism. Would Islam have its adherents denied the latest in cultural or scientific or technological innovations? Indeed one can live a devoutly religious life in a devoutly religious society while the devotee and the devout nation can fully participate in public secular life. Judaism, Christianity and

Islam share the understanding that the believer must participate, as a devoutly religious person, in all aspects of the public life of their nation and that their nation can be based on religious law and custom. The idea that the public advocacy by the believer of religious moral and ethical beliefs derived from their faith impinges upon freedom or discriminates against those of different faiths or the non-belief of the non-believer is a fiction that has been promulgated by non-believers who seek a monopoly of power. Islamic life and faith is potentially as compatible with the modern secular world as Judaism and Christianity have proven to be.

Islam is more vulnerable to the manipulations of modern Communism than is Christianity because Islam shares certain doctrines with Communism that tend to call for a regimented collectivized society, doctrines that call for the purging of those who fail to conform. Islam also shares with Communism a utopian demand for world conquest and world order. These principles form the bedrock and provide the raison deter of Communism but Islam is more nuanced and complex. While there should be no backing away from a vigorous critique of the dark side of Islam and Islamic doctrines, there nevertheless has been and remains an Islamic social order that maintains the rudiments of divinely inspired law. Muslims believe in God and Islam is consistent with the Covenant of Noah. Islam embraces the Torah, it recognizes the ministry of Jesus of Nazareth, it contains the basic structures of received morality and ethics, and it upholds rules of engagement in war. While Communism represents the principle of social and moral relativity, scarcity and death, and while Communism holds as the ultimate virtue the annihilation of the sovereign individual, who is merged into the brainless collectivist world ant colony, Islam holds that the individual is created in the image of Allah and is answerable to a higher authority. Islam holds to the hope and the possibility of individual redemption and progress. Communism does not.

The relatively laid back Islamic culture and political system that had been in place for over a millennia changed in 1915 with the launch of the coordinated Turkish Genocide against the Christian Armenian minority, a genocide that was launched by the radical secularist and anti-Islamic Young Turk government of the Three Pashas. Terror conducted in the name if Islam has ever since wracked Islamic countries, terror that has been exported into the non-Islamic world. It is the contention of this author that the change was due to the Communist influence originally emanating from Europe, the same Communist influence that began to transform the moral and social order of Europe itself during the 1793-1795 French Reign of Terror. The influence became manifest with the direct participation of the two European socialist experiments of the 20th Century, Nazi Socialism and Soviet Communism.

Thus, in many respects, Judaism Christianity and Islam have all been subverted to varying degrees by Communism. Certainly Communism has gone under different names at different times and under different circumstances but for the sake of brevity the term *Communism* is employed here as it provides the best catch-phrase for the ideology and the movement that subverted the conventional and natural modes of morality that were the norms in both the Judeo-Christian West and in the Islamic world. We will examine how Communism influenced Islam as a faith and how Communist groups, operating through subversion and aided and financed by wealthy westerners and western powers, gave rise to Islamic terror as we know it today.

The simple truth is that most of the radical Islamist groups and nations today are either Communist or Communist inspired. The Ba'ath Socialist movement, launched in the 1930's and inspired by Nazi socialism, became Communist after World War II and gave birth to the Communist regimes of Saddam Hussein in Iraq, the Assad regime in Syria, and that of the late Muammar Gaddafi in Libya. The Muslim Brotherhood and its offshoots, Hamas and Islamic Jihad, were and remains Communist. The revolutionary Iranian regime, from Ayatollah Khomeini to Ahmadinejad is a Communist regime. The Saudi Royal family is generally communistic in nature. Algeria is controlled by Communists. The war against Israel is a Communist war against a Capitalist society that threatens Communist hegemony. Al Qaeda and the 9/11 terrorists were all Communists.

The Soviet Union concluded, probably sometime in the 1960's, that Arabs and Muslims would not accept atheistic Communism outright so they devised a new Islamo-Communist faith that would take over Islamic and Arab lands and launch revolution, or "Jihad" against the Capitalist west. The Arab and Islamic Communists thus donned the garb and affected the mannerisms of traditional Islam. The new Islamo-Communism would isolate and magnify the most violent aspects of traditional Islam, those aspects which mirror Communism exactly, while stripping away the monotheistic belief in God and the moral code as shared by Judaism and Christianity. Many Islamo-Communists themselves are not conscious of the fact that they are actually Communists and that their faith has little resemblance, other than certain outward and cosmetic aspects, of traditional and normative Islam. The new Islamo-Communism would share with conventional Communism a shared goal of subjugating their populations and subduing the entire planet.

The Communists did not invent terror, atrocity, or political violence as the use of force and violence represent the dark side of human nature. The use of violence as a last resort when employed in defense of life and liberty is recognized as a universal right. Certainly nations have been involved in terrible atrocities, including Christian nations who have even committed atrocities in the name of their faith, and certainly war crimes have occurred in the void created by the heat of battle, but such atrocities are the exception and they are viewed as a disgrace. While western nations should do a better job of condemning the atrocities that they have committed, nevertheless such atrocities are contrary to accepted rules of engagement that go back to the Bible.

The rules of engagement regarding war were established in the Bible, rules that are recognized by Judaism, Christianity and Islam, and they pertain to the attack on the Israelite caravan by the Amelekites. The Amelekites attacked the Israelite caravan, made up of former slaves and led by Moses, from behind where there were women, children, the infirm and the elderly. Thus the cowardly Amelekites, engaging in the world's first act of terrorism, attacked the most vulnerable and defenseless members of the caravan. This was assumedly done by them as a means to demoralize the Israelites and to soften them up for battle.

The Talmudic Rabbis did not view the Amelekites as an ethnic group per se but rather as a group that had violated the most basic rules of engagement in war and, as such, had violated the basic fabric that constituted the social order. The Rabbis condemned the Amelekites of every generation and required the children of Israel to eradicate them before they turned human civilization into a barbarous condition of chaos. Islam like Christianity holds to the laws of the Torah and forbids terrorism, the murder of innocent women and children in the course of war, the wonton killing of the most vulnerable. This is not to say that there have not been incidences where Islamic forces and nations have committed such atrocities but when they have, such actions have been in violation of their faith which has served as a restraining influence. Christians have also violated these rules. One example that could be sited is the war between the New England Puritans and the natives, known as King Phillip's War, in which the Puritans, in the name of their faith, slaughtered entire native Indian villages.

The Communists brought terrorism to a new level. It is the Communist approach to terrorism that has infected the minds and the souls of both Christians and Muslims. It was the Communists who raised terror to the status of a great and indeed moral tactic to be conducted in the name of their perverted view of societal "progress." Never before in human history had a group reveled in and glorified in terrorism, the murder of the innocent. Indeed the Communists view terror as a necessary tactic to advance their agenda toward human collectivism. The red in the flag of Communism stands for the human blood that would have to be shed in order to affect the birth pangs of Socialism. There is not a page of Communist literature that is not soaked in violence which is glorified as part of the "struggle." There has never been a Communist movement or regime that has not sustained itself on the principle of ongoing violence against the innocent, what they consider to be "revolution." It was the Communist idea, the idea of evolving or advancing human society by eradicating those deemed to be regressive, that formed the moral justification for the highly organized form of terror that was conducted by the Nazis and by every Communist regime.

In my first book in this series, "The Nazi Connection to Islamic Terrorism" I elaborated upon the career of the peaceful and forward thinking Islamic Hashemite King of post-World War I Syria and Iraq Faisal ibn Hussein, and the agreement he signed as the Arab representative to the Paris Peace Conference recognizing Jewish Palestine. King Faisal's agreement, which was accepted by most forward thinking Arabs of his day, was largely scuttled by Haj Amin al-Husseini, the British appointed Mufti of Jerusalem during the British Mandate of Palestine. al-Husseini, who is considered to be the founder of the modern Palestinian movement along with his nephew Yasir Arafat, was a close collaborator of Hitler and a promoter of the Nazi Holocaust during World War II. It should be noted that there has been a curious and shameful history of western nations, starting with Great Britain, promoting the more radical Islamic leaders and ignoring the moderates.

It is easy for those of us living in the western democracies, especially due to current events regarding Islamic terrorism, to point an accusing finger Islam yet, it should be noted, it was the European enlightenment that gave birth to the two world conquering socialist movements, Nazism and Communism, movements responsible for more terror and death than any in world history. This book examines the extent to which the dark side of the European enlightenment and its Communist manifestation influenced the development of radical Islam. The first book in this series traced the influence of Nazi socialism on Islam by focusing on the personality and career of the infamous Mufti of Jerusalem Haj Amin al-Husseini. This book focuses specifically on the insidious influence of the modern Communist left on the rise of radical Islam from the early 19th Century up until the present day. It should be viewed as no coincidence that elements of the international Left today serve as apologists and defenders of radical Islam. We shall examine the cause of this seemingly strange and unholy alliance.

Two streams of thought and two streams of faith have run through Islamic history from the beginning. This is true even of the Koran itself which appears to be divided between a more peaceful and moral first half and a more militant and violent second half. In modern times the Nazis and the Soviets, two imports into the Islamic world, imports into the Islamic mind and soul, have been able to isolate the second half, effectively toss out the first half, and then magnify certain elements of the second half by isolating those elements from a greater context of faith and moral standards. The integration of both parts of Islam, and of the Koran has served as a natural check on unfettered assertiveness and power while leaving in place the principle of national and cultural determination.

The Nazis and Communists isolated the second half of Islam for their own self-serving reasons and the victim has been the Muslim people and Islam itself. Both the West and Islam would be well served by an expose of this subversive conspiracy with the hope that the two parts of Islam, torn asunder, might once again be united in a religion of peace, power, spirituality, sovereignty and prosperity for the Islamic faith and the Muslim people. Such an examination might serve the same purpose for the West as well.

Communism and Monotheism

Whittaker Chambers, the former American Communist spy who turned into one of the greatest witnesses against Communism in history described Communism in his seminal autobiography "Witness" as "man's second oldest faith" and the "great alternative faith of mankind." Chambers wrote "Its promise was whispered in the first days of the creation under the Tree of the Knowledge of Good and Evil: 'Ye shall be as gods." Thus the Communist replaces the received wisdom of the ages, the divine writ, and the sum total of human experience, millennia of trial and error, with the simple notion that man can and indeed must replace God and change human nature by simple virtue of the assumption that man, not God, is the foci of creation and is therefore the center of the universe.

Chambers wrote that Communism is animated by a simple conviction: "It is necessary to change the world." This same conviction is held by believers in the three great monotheistic faiths, this same messianic vision, but there is a very profound and important difference. The monotheists believe that changing the world requires an adherence by individuals and nations to a divinely set moral code, a code that exists outside of human control or manipulation. The Communists believe in Man as the creator of morality and justice and, as such, that an enlightened clique must assume the responsibility of serving as the scientific vanguard for the inferior masses. The monotheistic faiths view the end game, the Messianic age, as to be in the hands of a supernatural force. The Communist messianic utopia occurs when the enlightened elite evolves man, by means of force or fraud, into a superior animal that lives in peace and harmony unburdened by such false consciousness and superstitions as individual identity, faith, family, fidelity, honor, property and sovereignty.

The monotheistic process is positive, a personal belief in the creator and what is required to live the good life. The Communist process is negative in that it requires the annihilation of those individuals and nations that stand in the way of their man-made notion of human progress. The monotheist believes that good and evil exist and can be determined, the Communist believes that good and evil are relative to a man-made vision of progress and, essentially, that good and evil are self-interested creations by men conspiring to oppress and exploit their fellow men.

Monotheism establishes the foundations of individual freedom through immutable laws. Communism views the ultimate virtue to be a surrender of individual freedom in the interest of establishing an international ant colony by means of collectivism. Monotheism is natural as it is based upon the form of human organization that has proven to foster freedom and success, Communism is artificial as no man or nation has ever or would ever voluntarily submit to its dictates. This is why monotheism mostly spread peacefully and is adhered to by it followers willingly and voluntarily while Communism has only been able to exist at the point of a gun. Nations and societies founded on the monotheistic principles of Christianity and Islam have survived and, indeed progressed for thousands of years without interruption while Communist societies survive only until they run out of people and nations they can plunder.

Chambers poses the great proposition of the ages, one that has become particularly acute and urgent in our modern age of nuclear weapons and other weapons of mass destruction and that proposition is the choice between God and Man. The Bible instructs us that men and women were created in the image of God and, as such, were not gods. This biblical passage recognizes that man is imperfect and will never be perfected. Communism seeks to make human beings and societies perfect which is why one might hear communist minded people speak of "ending" poverty, crime, hunger, disease, war, and any other miserable condition that human beings and societies find themselves mired in from time to time. Indeed, the calling card of Communism is that the Communists, by will of mind and action, can make the world perfect and, as such, end all human suffering. The Communist feels aided in this pursuit by a misinterpretation of the goals of science.

Mankind and human societies are not perfect and will never be made perfect short of a divine intervention. We can make the world a better place by embracing freedom enhancing structures, engaging in hospitality and acts of kindness, and by helping others in need. This is, indeed, a central tenet of the monotheistic faiths. The imperfectness of man, which is a reflection of the human condition, has resulted in inevitable mistakes and errors that have seeped into the lives of every person and society and this includes the monotheistic religions themselves. In this regard, Islam made a mistake in its doctrine, a mistake that does not exist in either Judaism or Christianity. That doctrine is a call for the followers of the Prophet Muhammad to physically conquer the entire world by any means necessary, persuasion, subterfuge, coercion or war. It is this Islamic doctrine of Jihad that precisely mirrors the Communist doctrine and this is partially why Muslims have been vulnerable to the tender ministrations of the Communist "revolution."

Judaism aspires only to possess that tiny and inscrutable speck of land that lies between the Jordan River and the Mediterranean Sea, the Land of Israel. This Jewish doctrine is also recognized in the holy books of both Christianity and Islam. Christianity seeks adherents across the globe but only as an act of voluntary conversion as the underlying principle of Christianity is the establishment of a personal and voluntary relationship between the believing Christian and Jesus Christ. Historically, Christians have violated this tenet of their faith on many occasions but, nevertheless, those violations run contrary to Christian doctrine and, indeed, are more representative of the secular and earthly influences of ambitious men and corrupt governments.

The ancient idea of Communism is, at its core, a denial of basic and discernible truths both material as well as spiritual. If man is to "be as gods" than man is the creator of the universe. As such, man creates truths and, in the literal sense, man invents reality. Nothing is therefore objective or true but only subjective and invented. Nothing is definable and fixed in its identity as everything is in a state of flux. For the Communist, nothing is real. Rather than recognizing the existence of set and identifiable abstract principles, for the Communist everything is in a state of evolution and the Communist feels he has the ability to re-invent himself every day. Communism claims to hold the keys to abolishing "false consciousness" yet Communism itself if demonstrably a false consciousness. Yet the appeal of Communism is obvious. To the individual, Communism offers an opportunity to shape, re-shape, and invent basic truths. To the nation, as a governing philosophy, Communism offers a moral and practical patina to totalitarianism.

Communism has thus always been and remains the governing philosophy of power, authority, dictatorship, and total government. How else could governing enlightened elites be able to change reality than through the force of government? The proof of the un-natural nature of the Communist enterprise, active government run by a revolutionary enlightened elite charged with the moral responsibility to change mankind, is that no such government has ever existed or can exist except at the point of a gun. This is because the individual will never surrender his naturel, objective and self-evident rights. Among those rights, as Thomas Jefferson wrote in the Declaration of Independence, are "life, liberty and the pursuit of happiness."

Thus Communism is an ancient idea and a movement that has reared its head in human society from the very beginning of recorded human history. Friedrich Engles, the wealthy Capitalist who supported Marx financially and who was his chief collaborator, wrote of "primitive Communism" as a condition of man living off the land before the development of money, class structure and government. Because there was no "surplus capital" in pre-historic times, man had not yet developed the concept of private property, government, or trade, as everything save the shirt on his back was collectively owned due to the sheer need to survive. Engles contended, and rightfully, that man developed "class society" with the development of agriculture and animal domestication which replaced hunting and gathering. Other factors that furthered human societal development in the direction away from primitive Communism were improvements in science, art, culture, architecture and the establishment of cities which required organization in terms of the division of property, the ability to trade in goods and services and an abstract means of conducting that trade, money, and political organization, hence sovereign governments.

As man began to utilize means to organize a growing and increasingly complex society, due to various developments associated with the emergence of civilization, man ditched primitive Communism. Yet, at the same time Marx and Engles were correct to note that as man emerged, man began to exploit his fellow man in various ways including the development of slavery, human sacrifice and war. Marx theorized that such exploitation increased as man advanced until in modern times which, according to Marx, man existed in a state of exploitation and informal slavery of one portion of society by another. Thus Marx presented his theory of exploitation and class conflict.

Yet the idea that by re-imposing the ancient principle of Communism, which Engles had correctly pointed out was the condition of Man before that dawn of civilization, would end exploitation is insane and is an entirely materialistic view of humanity. Accompanying the emergence from primitive Communism and into civilization, and accompanying the negative aspects of that emergence, exploitation, slavery, war, human sacrifice, also emerged the countervailing influence of the rule of law, individual identity, faith, and ideas and institutions that would point man in the direction of freedom and a more moral society.

The Bible and other ancient documents such as the Code of Hammurabi, pointed to law that were outside human manipulation, law that would define morality and would provide a blueprint for progress. The Bible pointed man in the direction of eventually abolishing slavery and the Bible did abolish human sacrifice. The Bible established an organized means of separation of individuals, property, and nations in such a way as to infuse these ideas, natural to humanity, with a moral content that would allow individuals and nations to prosper. The Bible established, by means of this concept of separation and the sacredness of every single human being, concepts of moral and sexual restraint. The Bible established the laws of nations and the rules of engagement concerning war.

Thus the Bible points man in the direction away from exploitation by establishing the rule of law while recognizing the imperfectness of man and the reality that human beings, while born equal and while entitled to equal rights and dignities, are nevertheless de facto unequal in terms of abilities, skill levels, and other circumstances. By establishing the core principles of rule of law beyond human manipulation, the Bible sets the stage for unequal individuals to live together in relative harmony and for society to advance through the inventiveness and creativity that can only occur in a context in which the individual is free to think and to work voluntarily with other likeminded individuals toward a common purpose.

From the dawn of civilization to modern times Communist movements, which have emerged under different names and under guises tailored to match specific conditions and cultures, have surfaced in all nations and amongst all peoples. They have always, without exception, utilized the deception that is inherent in a conspiracy that is cultivated within a secret society. They have always sought to overthrow the existing order by means of subversion and often by means of violence and force. They have always held out the promise to the population at large that they would end "exploitation" by seizing the property of the "exploiter" and this would lead to freedom and a more distributive prosperity. They have always held as an ideal a return to primitive Communism in the form of modern Collectivism where property would be abolished and "surplus capital" would be distributed "according to need." Those with ability would work for those in need for the "common good." Such "false consciousness" as property, faith, family, trade, and 'self-interest' would be, as Marx wrote "swept away and made impossible."

Without exception, every Communist movement, from ancient times until the present, has been controlled and financed by the richest members of society. Perhaps this is due to a misplaced sense of guilt for success, a sense especially held by many of inherited wealth. Perhaps the individual of material means, whether earned or inherited, feels the urge to step beyond mere material comfort and to use the fruits of that success to obtain power over others, to change the world so to speak. This ilk, those who control vast fortunes who are oriented in this way have, without exception, walked away from or never held a traditional belief in God or a fixed moral code. They seek to replace God, or fill the void in their own souls, by seeking to assume the role of an earthly God as they seek to steward over their fellows with what they feel is an enlightened knowledge and for their own good. This temptation, to play God on earth, has always been too intoxicating a temptation for many of those of wealth to resist. In modern times, this is why the wealthiest class financed, supported, and literally made possible the two biggest utopian Communist experiments of the 20th Century, Sovietism and Nazism.

Islam, unlike Judaism and Christianity, is a faith that was founded by a man who was both a spiritual as well as a political and military leader. The Prophet Muhammad was both the spiritual founder of the faith as well as the military conqueror and ruler of most of Arabia at the time of his death. This principle has made Islam more vulnerable to the temptation of Communism than has been Christianity. Islam as a faith has a more explicitly political and military nature than does Christianity. Both religions embrace aspirations of world control but in the case of Islam this is more easily translated into literal political and military terms while Christianity is more oriented toward missionizing and the encouragement of a personal relationship between the individual and Christ. When Christian nations have engaged in military conquest in the name of their faith they are actually contradicting their faith. The same cannot be said of Islam which is why the earthly and authoritarian aspect of Islam has tended to find common cause with the completely earthly and authoritarian Communist endeavor.

After the death of the Prophet Muhammad, 632 AD, his generals proceeded to conquer the Middle East, Egypt, Persia, and North Africa. In subsequent centuries Islamic forces conquered most of northern Africa, much of Spain, Asia Minor, and the Balkans up to the gates of Vienna and southern Poland. Muslims moved east through India, Indonesia, and the southern Philippines. They solidified their position in Afghanistan and Central Asia. Militant Islam remains a political and military force today which threatens the western democracies.

Expansionism was by no means unique to Islam as Christian nations were on the march particularly in the 19th and early 20th Centuries as Christian Europe, particularly Britain and France, established colonies in populated regions of Africa and Asia. While Islamic pirates roamed the Mediterranean seizing ships and enslaving Europeans, seizures which led President Jefferson to send the Marines to the shores of Tripoli, European pirates, at times casually affiliated with the British, roamed the Atlantic and both Muslim and European slave traders shipped chattel slaves to the new world. Europe attempted to subjugate and colonize Arab and Islamic nations starting with Napoleon's invasion of Egypt in 1799 and the French establishment of a colony in Algeria in 1830. European meddling in the Arab world accelerated after World War I with the division of Middle Eastern Ottoman lands between Britain and France.

The Communist Takeover of the Ottoman Empire

The most significant Islamic nation for over five centuries until modern times was unquestionably the Ottoman Empire. The Turkic Ottomans had established themselves in Asia Minor for over a century when in 1453 Mehmed II conquered Constantinople and assumed the title of Roman Emperor, a title that was never recognized by the Christian west. The Ottoman Islamic Caliphate was thus established 39 years before Christopher Columbus set sail for the New World. That Empire ceased to exist in the aftermath of World War I when, on March 3, 1924, the Caliphate was formally abolished and the Republic of Turkey was proclaimed. The Greek Orthodox patriarch of Constantinople recognized Ottoman authority in 1453 in exchange for Ottoman recognition of the autonomous office of patriarch and the retention by the Greek Orthodox Church of authority and church properties.

For over five centuries the Ottomans maintained sovereign control over a region that at times stretched from Algeria to the border of Persia, from the southern border of Poland to the Gulf of Aden and near the source of the Nile and even as far away as Aceh on the Island of Sumatra in Indonesia. The Arabian Peninsula was essentially a vassal of the Ottoman Empire with the Ottomans controlling Mecca and Medina, the two Holy cities of Islam.

Ottoman armies twice threatened Vienna while maintaining control of the Crimea, Yemen, and the Persian Gulf coast of Arabia. Ottoman navies commanded the eastern Mediterranean and the Black Sea. Much has been written analyzing why the Ottomans and Ottoman society fell behind Europe in terms of cultural and economic development. It should be noted that, nevertheless, the Ottomans maintained a vast and diverse empire under relatively peaceful and prosperous conditions for over 5 Centuries. The Sunni Ottoman Turks were generally tolerant, religiously moderate, and more cohesive and peaceful than the bickering European states which were often at war with each other during those centuries.

The 19th Century was known as the Tanzimat or reorganization period in Ottoman Turkey. This was a time when the best aspects of European and American culture and science made significant inroads. Industrialization, infrastructure development, constitutional limits on the Sultanate, the brief establishment of a Parliament, modern banking, post offices, public education and advances in art and architecture were all the hallmarks of this century in Turkey. While the 19th Century was a time of political and military decline for the Ottomans, as the empire retreated from the Balkans and elsewhere, the Empire nevertheless moved in the direction of a modern state based upon the best democratic principles.

Modern Communists have always operated in secret societies. This is probably true regarding pre-modern Communists as well. The nature of Communism requires a high degree of secrecy and deception for the obvious reason that Communists seek to subvert and overthrow governments. The less obvious reason for this necessity is that Communists, in order to affect their revolutionary goals and their long-term change in human nature, must deceive the masses. The end goal of Communism, a world collectivist beehive, is a goal that no sane person would ever voluntarily agree to which is why the Communists must plan and plot, in secret, the means to market and sell their wares to enough people. Communism depends on violence, chaos, and social disruption as the catalyst for change. The unnatural goals of Communism must, by nature, involve secrecy.

An excellent and authoritative source on the modern history of Communist, Communist infiltrated and Communist aligned European secret societies is "Fire in the Minds of Men – Origins of the Revolutionary Tradition" by James H. Billington, published 1980. The liberal Billington, one of America's most esteemed scholars and academics, was appointed as Librarian of Congress in 1987. In this seminal book, Billington thoroughly documents Communist action, as conducted through secret societies, in the fomenting of revolution and authoritarianism in Europe from the founding of the Illuminati by Adam Weishaupt in 1776 to the Bolshevik Coup of 1917. Billington reveals the meaning of the left-wing French slogan "Liberty, Fraternity, Equality" which is generally associated with the freedom oriented French Revolution. Liberty, Billington notes, stands for the conventional form of Liberty that drove the American Revolution, Fraternity is the concept that gave birth to Fascism and Nazism, movements based upon the socialistic and collective principles of hyper-nationalism and racial collectivism, and Equality represents the far left-wing Communist conception as it was articulated by the Bolsheviks.

The Young Turkish National Movement, formed in the late 19th Century, launched the Young Turk uprising on March 31, 1908. The result was that Ottoman Sultan Abdul Hamid II stepped down on April 27, 1909. Sultan Abdul Hamid II, who was a devout Muslim and who adhered to Islamic codes of morality, had introduced many genuinely progressive reforms over a 40 year rule that was marked by stability tolerance and peace. The new Young Turk government that replaced Abdul Hamid and turned his successor, Mehmed V into a figurehead, systematically dismantled the Ottoman Empire by first surrendering Ottoman Balkan lands and then disastrously aligning with Imperial Germany in World War I. Austria-Hungary took advantage of the instability associated with the 1908 uprising by seizing Muslim majority Bosnia and Herzegovina. Two additional Balkan wars led to Ottoman defeat and atrocities against Muslim Turks and Albanians initiated by Serbia.

 The Committee of Union and Progress was a secret society that partially subverted what might have otherwise been a democratic and progressive Young Turk revolution. The Young Turk National Movement itself stood for religious freedom, limited constitutional government, industrial progress, and national independence and most of its supporters expected Ottoman Turkey to develop along the lines of democratic Europe and America. It has been generally assumed in Turkey that the CUP benefited from operating within Turkish Masonic lodges that maintained associations with left controlled Masonic lodges in Europe. While such speculation is beyond the scope of this book, it should be noted that a strong distrust of Masonry exists in Turkey today due to this understanding.

Abdullah Cevdet, one of the founders of the secretive CUP, was described by Princeton historian Şükrü Hanioğlu as having been "deeply influenced by the German vulgar materialism of late 19th century, which heralded a post-religious world solely guided by "science and reason." Cevdet, who could be described as the theoretician of the CUP, was disliked by the Turkish people for his anti-Islamic tracts published in newspapers he edited. Cevdet was an admirer of the Darwinian progressive "science" of eugenics and, as such, Cevdet contributed in introducing racist and ethno-centric politics into Turkey where it did not exist before. It should be understood that eugenics, initiated by Charles Darwin's cousin and collaborator British scientist Francis Galton, was viewed as progressive in western circles until the end of World War II. Eugenics sought to evolve the human species through superior breeding.

In 1913, after the Young Turks had suffered a series of military defeats that resulted in Ottoman Turkey surrendering all of its European territory, the coup of the CUP Three Pashas moved the nation further to the left in terms of setting in place a one party state that would be viewed as inseparable from the state itself. The Three Pashas, Mehmed Taalat Ismail Enver, and Ahmed Djemal, strengthened the grip of the anti-Islamic CUP, further marginalized the Sultan and consolidated power into the hands of a centralized dictatorship. Their government was Islam's first totalitarian regime and it was inspired by western ideas such as Marxism.

On April 24, 1915, Talaat issued the order to close all Armenian political organizations and to arrest all Armenians associated with those organizations. This action led to the Armenian Genocide in which an estimated 1 to 2 million Armenian men women and children were brutally and systematically murdered or marched to their deaths through starvation. Enver, the military member of the Junta during World War I initiated the policy of relocating Armenians and other Christians. This genocidal policy was based upon Enver's false claim that Armenian soldiers were responsible for his terrible defeats on the Turkish-Russian front. Enver scapegoated Turkish Christians for his own incompetence and confiscated their lands and wealth. Enver and his fellow Junta members signed a treaty of friendship with Lenin and the Bolsheviks on January 1, 1918.

The three Pashas fled into exile at the end of the war. Enver was sentenced to death in absentia for policies that led to the Armenian Genocide. After meeting high-level Bolshevik Karl Radek in Berlin, Enver went to Moscow where he met Lenin and was named head of the Soviet Asiatic Department. After attending the Communist "Congress of Eastern Peoples" in Baku, September 1-8, 1920, Enver travelled to Berlin where he attempted to establish a group that would transfer Soviet aid to Turkey presumably to assist a Soviet backed Communist takeover. The Congress of Eastern Peoples was primarily attended by Central Asian representatives of nations that were fighting Soviet forces. An example of the rhetoric heard at the conference was that of Dagestan Communist Jalalad'din Korkmasov who declared that a: *heroic struggle... has dyed Dagestan in the color of its own blood, shed for the glorious Red Flag... what is at stake is the world revolution. What faces us is a great world war... even before the [Baku] Congress... before the call issued by our leaders we began a holy war.*

In November, 1921, Lenin sent Enver to the Central Asian Turkestan Soviet Republic to assist in the quelling of the anti-Soviet Basmachi rebellion, a rebellion that actually began in 1915 in reaction to the Russian Tsar's attempt at forced conscription into the Russian Army. Enver switched sides and became commander of the Basmachi forces fighting the Soviets. After losing the support of local Muslim leaders, Enver died in a Soviet ambush on August 4, 1922. Clearly the Soviets, as early as 1918, were cultivating Muslim contact in Islamic lands for the purpose of subversion by establishing secret groups such as the one that Enver attempted to establish under Soviet sponsorship.

In many ways the leftist CUP overthrow in 1908 mirrored every other Communist takeover of a nation since the French Reign of Terror subversion of the French Revolution of 1789. First the Communist secret society, in this case the CUP, assists in a bloodless takeover of the old regime, in this case that of Abdul Hamid II after a period of intense propaganda and demonization of the leader. The well-meaning participants in the takeover, an event that was effected mostly by people who sought to establish genuinely progressive freedom oriented change, are then subverted by the Communist secret society, in this case the CUP. The said secret society often receives various levels of material and propaganda support from international fellow-traveling groups. The coup, affected in a manufactured atmosphere of emergency and crisis, then seizes the reins of government as did, in this case, the Three Pashas. The new government, in this case that of the Three Pasha Junta, than quickly consolidates power, in the name of "the people," in order to solve the manufactured emergency crisis.

The results of the conspiracy vary depending on the specifics conditions existing within the targeted country. In the case of Ottoman Turkey, the result was a powerful dictatorship the likes of which the Islamic world had never experienced. This is not to say that the Islamic world was by any means liberal and democratic by the standards of today. The Communist conspiracy in Ottoman Turkey reversed a trend toward liberalism begun in the 19th Century during the Tanzimat era, a trend that was compatible with Islam and that was moving toward greater tolerance of religious minorities. The Communist influence within the otherwise democratic Young Turk Movement, and the Communist Coup of the Three Pashas, retarded that organic growth and created a totalitarian state based on Communist as opposed to genuinely liberal principles.

The dictatorship of the Three Pashas dragged Turkey into military defeat in World War I, a senseless bloodbath and a devastating war. The anti-Islamic Pashas launched the largest program of coordinated Genocide the world had ever known up until that point. In classic Communist fashion, they confiscated the property of those they murdered and they set in place policies that restricted private ownership, centralized the power of the total state, and contracted the basic freedoms of its citizens. Islam was not responsible for the Genocide against the Armenians. The Communist oriented Pashas who subverted Islam were responsible for the Armenian Genocide.

Islam was no more to blame for the Armenian Genocide than Christianity was to blame for the Nazi Holocaust. The Three Pashas, like Hitler, were anti-religious radical secular leaders. Both movements, the CUP and the Nazis, were secular and anti-religious. Both movements sought to eradicate their perceived opponents, those to whom they claimed stood in the way of their twisted idea of social progress. Both movements utilized a degree of religious rhetoric to justify their agenda to their people. Both the Armenians in Ottoman Turkey and the Jews in Germany represented and in many ways embodied principles that were obstacles to the Communist agendas of the CUP and the Nazis and those were a developed sense of individualism, a high level of education, and a significant degree of financial success. Both the CUP and the Nazis expropriated wealth and property from the Armenians and the Jews, re-distributing these to "the people."

Mustapha Kemal Ataturk, the founder of the Republic of Turkey in 1924, saved his country in the aftermath of the Three Pasha defeat in a manner that was similar to the way Napoleon Bonaparte saved France in the aftermath of the Reign of Terror. Ataturk was a military man, the only man standing after the defeat of Turkey at the end of World War I. Ataturk had started out as a member of the CUP but once in power he abolished the organization. He worked with the Bolsheviks in his effort to drive out the Allied occupiers after the war, particularly in his brutal war against Greece, but Ataturk, once firmly in power, put the Bolshevik Communists on notice by arranging for the murder of the Turkish Communist Party leadership. While Ataturk was no Communist, he certainly could be described as to the left of the governments of the old Islamic Ottoman Caliphate in terms of his centralization of power but he was to the right of the more radical Three Pashas.

It would be simplistic to claim that Ataturk, who ruled Turkey 1925-1938, was anti-Islamic. Ataturk was, first and foremost, a military tactician but he was also a Turkish patriot, a secularist and a pragmatist. He wanted Islam to become modern in the sense that he believed in a separation of Mosque and State and he required that Muslims accept European culture. He banned secret societies turning them into social clubs and their buildings into museums. He insisted on absolute sovereignty for his country, and freedom of religion, but he sought to ally Turkey with Europe politically and culturally. He maintained neutrality and he disavowed terror as a tactic to be used against his neighbors. While Ataturk presided over a strong centralized state, his vision was not comparable to that of his predecessors, the three Pashas, nor was it comparable to the totalitarian Socialism of the Soviet Union or the emerging totalitarian socialist systems of his contemporary nations in Europe, Fascist Italy and Nazi Germany.

Mustafa Kemal Ataturk abolished the Ottoman Caliphate on March 3, 1924. On that date, Ataturk sent Abdulmecid II out of his office in Constantinople and into exile. The office of the Caliphate was comparable to that of the office of the Pope of the Roman Catholic Church. The first Caliph, by Islamic tradition, was the Prophet Mohammad and the office was then held by a long line of leaders who assumed both religious and temporal powers. The office changed in many ways over the millennia of its existence but the office remained the foci of Islam both spiritually and politically. The Caliph was in a position to render religious decisions that would serve Islam in the context of the times in which he served.

The office of the Ottoman Caliphate in particular represented a high point for Islam. The Ottoman Caliph was not only the head of the vast Ottoman land but also wielded religious authority in Central Asia, India, Indonesia, Africa, and in other regions and communities outside the empire that were in the Sunni Muslim tradition. The Caliph also was held in esteem among Shia Muslims. By the time Ataturk abolished the Caliphate, the political power of the Caliph had largely been transferred to the Turkish Republic headed by Araturk yet the religious significance and influence of the office of Caliph remained intact throughout the Islamic world.

Ataturk made a terrible mistake when he abolished the office of the Caliph. The Caliph served as a central and respected figure that could make binding decisions on Islam in the same way that the Pope makes decisions for the Catholic Church. The result has been that Islam has been in a period of spiritual disunity and, to a certain extent political drift ever since. The stabilizing presence of the Caliph has been replaced by the destabilizing presence of corrupted Islamo-Communists such as Osama bin Laden. Since the loss of the office of Caliph, the radicals have been in a position to interpret the theoretical role of the Caliph to fit their image. This would not have been possible had a real Caliph been in place.

Ataturk carried on a modern tradition that was launched by Lenin and that has always been a main component of the Communist experiment and that was the elevation of the political leader into the status of a virtual deity. The Communists sought to replace God with the State and the Communist leader stood in as a surrogate God and as a focus of veneration. Lenin developed cult worship of the great leader and, on his death, he was deified in imitation of the rituals developed by the ancient Egyptians. Lenin's mummified body still lays in state in the Kremlin. Ataturk was set up in Turkey as almost a demigod in a manner that was too typical of many of the heads of state who assumed power in Lenin's wake.

The most notorious leader to utilize this principle started by Lenin and furthered by Stalin was Adolf Hitler who brought the concept, the "Fuhrerprincep" to the most lethal level ever previously attempted in history. Hitler's deification included the total manipulation of all media to the point that sensory perception was tinkered with in an unprecedented way. Hitler's deification was brought to a level that resulted in the virtual brainwashing of an entire country. Other leaders of the 20th Century who attempted versions of the Furherprincep included Benito Mussolini in Italy, Francisco Franco in Spain, and, to certain degrees in within the context of limitations of western political and cultural traditions, Franklin D. Roosevelt, Winston Churchill, and after the war, Charles DeGaulle.

Leader deification and worship is an inherent part of the Communist ideology as it is necessary as a means to maintain the fraud that is total government. The Communist leader becomes the leader of progress, the hero of the people, and the great and glorious champion of science. The Communist leader delivers his people from the manufactured emergency. Every Communist country without exception has been based on the principle of the Furherprincip. The worst examples of this principle in action include Mao tse Tung, Fidel Castro, Ho Chi Minh, Kim Ill Sung, and lesser Communist potentates including Marshall Tito and Nicolai Chauchescu. Every Islamo-Communist state since World War II has been based on the Communist Furherprincip as such leaders include Sadaam Hussein, Hafez al-Assad, Abdul Gamal Nasser, Muammar el-Gaddafi, the Ayatollah Ruhollah Khomeini, and several lesser potentates. Many leaders in Africa and Asia have tried to emulate the Fuhrerprincep with different degrees of success.

In every case, without exception, the existence of the enthroned Communist leader is accompanied by poverty and the loss of freedom. The furherprincip was alien to the Islamic world and was rejected by the western democracies. The Communists resurrected the old idea of the divine right of Kings. The American President is elected and has powers limited by the Constitution. The idea of the divine ruler is contrary to the three monotheistic faiths. The Prophet Samuel, recognized by the three faiths, warned the Israelites of the dangers attendant to their desire to have a King:

I Samuel 8 (10-18) KJV:

10 And Samuel told all the words of the LORD unto the people that asked of him a king.

11 And he said, This will be the manner of the king that shall reign over you: He will take your sons, and appoint them for himself, for his chariots, and to be his horsemen; and some shall run before his chariots.

12 And he will appoint him captains over thousands, and captains over fifties; and will set them to ear his ground, and to reap his harvest, and to make his instruments of war, and instruments of his chariots.

13 And he will take your daughters to be confectionaries, and to be cooks, and to be bakers.

14 And he will take your fields, and your vineyards, and your olive yards, even the best of them, and give them to his servants.

¹⁵ And he will take the tenth of your seed, and of your vineyards, and give to his officers, and to his servants.

¹⁶ And he will take your menservants, and your maidservants, and your goodliest young men, and your asses, and put them to his work.

¹⁷ He will take the tenth of your sheep: and ye shall be his servants.

¹⁸ And ye shall cry out in that day because of your king which ye shall have chosen you; and the LORD will not hear you in that day.

Communism and Iran

Persia maintained a distinct culture and language after the Islamic conquest. Persia developed Shi'a, a distinctive form of Islam. Persia proved to possess a highly resilient culture which absorbed the many invaders of its lands including the Turks and the brutal 13ᵗʰ Century waves of Mongol hoards who slaughtered millions of Persians. Like the Ottomans, the Persians maintained a nation that was generally tolerant, moderately religious and relatively peaceful.

There is evidence that Persia experienced a Communist revolution over a century before the 7th Century Islamic conquest, a revolution that probably reverberates within Iranian society to this day. What is known is that a cult leader named Mazdak won the confidence of the Sassanid Persian King Kavadh I who ruled Persia 488-531. King Kavadh perhaps looked upon Mazdak as an agent in his quest to defeat his enemies and confiscate the wealth and property of the nobles in his kingdom. Mazdak, who became the equivalent of Prime Minister for a number of years, attempted to collectivize property and transfer wealth, in typical Communist fashion, transferring the loot to his allies and himself and probably sending the victims off to their deaths in the name of "the people" and as "enemies of the state." Persia predictably suffered as production fell off and, as is usually the case with Communist experiments; real poverty ensued once the expropriated wealth was blown.

Mazdak sought government control over Zoroastrianism, the partially monotheistic religion of Sassanid Persia. In a pattern that would be followed by future Communist experiments, Mazdak closed most Zoroastrian places of worship leaving only three open and under state control. Another characteristic of Mazdak was is pretensions as Messiah. Most Communist movements since, both religious and secular, involved a pseudo-Messiah or cult leader that derived their claim to super enlightenment either from a divine source or from their alleged superior scientific knowledge. Mazak, like his spiritual and ideological sucessors, claimed the power to define morality and actively advocated the overthrow of traditional moral nostrums as a means of advancing society. In Masdak's case this meant wife swapping.

Christian communistic messianic pretenders such as Peter the Hermit inspired the more violent side of the Crusades. Pseudo-Jewish Messiah Shabtai Zvi in the 17th Century and Jacob Frank in the 18th Century claimed divine powers that they alleged enabled them respectively to invalidate the moral and ethical precepts of the Torah. The secular Messiah's, the heroes of the revolution, Karl

Marx, Vladimir Lenin, Josef Stalin, Adolf Hitler, Mao tse Tung, Pol Pot, Ho Chi Minh, and a list of other rogues claimed the "scientific" power to use the earthly power of the state to change human nature in defiance of conventional tenets of morality.

Conditions deteriorated so severely in Persia under the guidance of Mazdak that King Kavadh was overthrown in 496. Kavadh made a comeback and was restored to the throne with the help of Mar Zutra II, the Jewish Exilarch of Persia who rose up against Mazdak who had sought to annihilate the Jews of Persia. Mar Zutra II, an observant Jew and the head of the great Talmudic academy at Pumbeditha in Persian Babylon, was nevertheless defeated by Mazdak after seven years of fighting. Mar Zutra was crucified by the forces of Mazdak on the same day as the birth of his son, Mar Zutra III who was taken to Israel, under Byzantine control, where he grew up to become head of the Talmudic Academy at Tiberius and the father of a long dynasty of Jewish scholars.

19th Century Persia was caught up in the "Great Game" competition between the British and Russian imperialists, both of whom infringed upon Persian sovereignty politically and economically. Motivated by the corruption and misrule of Mozaffar al-Din Shah Qajar, the 5th Qajar Shah of Persia, 1896-1907, a Constitutional movement developed under the influence of the merchant class. This was a genuinely middle class movement, with parallels to the American movement for independence which culminated in the US Constitution. In 1907, Mozaffar al-Din signed the Constitution which established government *under the rule of law, and the crown became a divine gift given to the Shah by the people.* This was the first Constitution adopted by an Asian nation and, for the first time the power of the King was limited and the King derived his authority as a gift given by the people. The Persian constitution was consistent with Shia Islam as the locus of authority was with the "Hidden Imam." This idea was not unlike the American conception, as expressed in the American Declaration of Independence, which spoke of rights, or governing authority, as derived from the creator. The Persian Constitution established an elected Parliament or Majlis.

The Shah died five days after signing the constitution into law and his son and successor, Mohammad Ali Shah Qajar, proceeded to dismiss the Majlis, bomb the Parliament building and suspend the Constitution. This was followed by over a decade of national weakness, intrigue, instability, tribal conflict and foreign interference. In this atmosphere of increasing lawlessness and with British and Tsarist Russian troops moving into the country in response to the discovery of oil, a constitutional movement developed in 1914, the Nehzat-e- Jangal or the Forest Movement. This movement, headed by Kuchik Khan, who was not a Communist and who is viewed as a national hero in Iran, was centered in the Gilani province on the coast of the Caspian Sea.

The Jangal movement, working with the conservative Society of Islamic Union, began an uprising in 1914 in the northern region around the Caspian Sea where they battled local warlords and Tsarist Russian troops. Their goal was to re-establish the constitution. The Bolsheviks in 1918 began to supply the Jangals who had experienced military setbacks. At the same time the Bolsheviks predictably began to infiltrate and take over the Jagual movement with their own well placed people operating from within. In May, 1920, Kuchik Khan declared an independent and separate Persian Socialist Soviet Republic in Gilan Province. Kuchik naïvely agreed to this move after receiving Soviet guarantees that they would provide military support but not intervene in the internal affairs of the new Republic which Kuchik viewed as a step toward liberating all of Persia from tyranny.

Kuchak's second in command, Ehsaonollah Khan and most of his cabinet were open Communists. Disagreement immediately surfaced between Kuchak and the more conservative members of the government and the Communists controlled by Moscow who wanted to seize all private property and agitate against Islam. Kuchak, who depended on his field commander Major von Pashen, had formed an alliance with Germany. Kuchak fled in June 1920 leaving the Kremlin minion Ehsaonollah and his Communist stooges in charge. They proceeded to predictably introduce a level of totalitarianism and violence into the region that had not been experienced since the 14th Century Mongol invasion of Timurlane. The Persian Soviet collapsed a year later amidst its utter rejection by "the people" and its abandonment by the Kremlin which chose to cut its losses in order to attempt to influence in Persia by other means.

In April, 1921, a successful coup in Tehran, led by General Reza Shah Pahlavi, signed a treaty with the Soviet Union which withdrew militarily from Persian soil. Reza Shah, who exiled Ahmad Shah Qajar and who himself became Shah in 1925, re-established the constitution, the Majlis, elections, and accepted a limited constitutional crown. Similarities exist between Reza Shah, who ruled 1925-1941, and his contemporary Turkish leader Mustapha Kemal Ataturk. Both rulers were secular anti-Communist strongmen who modernized their country but left Islam intact. Reza Shah championed the rights of women, he emancipated the Jews of Persia, and he introduced western political ideas, technology and culture into his country. In 1935, Reza Shah notified the League of Nations that his nation would be known by its ancient name of Iran. It has been suggested that he might have been motivated in this act by a possible admiration of the crackpot race theories of his contemporaries, the Nazis, as Iran means "land of the Aryans."

Nazism unleashed upon the firmament of humanity an evil form of socialism that proved in its lethality and toxicity to overpower the evil of its predecessor Soviet Communism. Nazism combined the French Revolution nostrums of Fraternity and Equality as the Nazis added race, inspired by Darwin's biological theory of human advancement, or fraternity, to Marx designation of class as the obstacle to human progress. Thus, as was the case with the Nazi view of the Jew, Marx analysis of Judaism as a class of "hucksters" who had to be eliminated to remove "hucksterism" from human society as "hucksterism" was a boulder blocking the road to human collectivism, the Nazi's added racist biological theory on top of Marx theory which the Nazis accepted wholeheartedly.

Resa Shah was a progressive economic nationalist in that he established for his country a national bank, a national railway system, public education, postal services, and other institutions of a modern sovereign nation. In the mid 1930's, Reza Shah became increasingly autocratic and corrupt as he tried to balance the ongoing

"Great Game" between the British and the Soviets by forming alliances with other nations, particularly Nazi Germany. Iran had cultivated relations with Germany going back to the turn of the century and the Shah viewed Germany as a counterbalance to the meddling of both the Soviets and the British. The Soviets and the British were direct threats to Iran as the Soviets posed a very real military and subversive threat while the British worked to loot Iran of its natural oil resources.

Indeed most of the Arab and Islamic world supported the Nazi regime to varying degrees in the early years, before its true nature had been fully revealed, as did much of what would later be referred to as the third world. Even the Roosevelt Administration openly admired Fascist Italy and was generally favorable to Nazi Germany in the early years of the regime. Several factors are attributable to this affinity which, it should be noted, was an affinity for Nazi Germany that existed before the World War of 1939 and the Holocaust against the Jews. Bolshevism, which had attained power in 1917, was a known evil and Bolshevik Communism was despised in the Arab and Islamic world. The Fascists and the Nazis were viewed as a power standing up to the Bolsheviks who, as was widely known, were responsible for the murders of 4 to 5 million people before 1920 and who had created the most oppressive regime ever known to human history up until that time. Lenin had already wiped out millions of innocent people before 1920, several years before Nazism had gotten off the ground.

The other perceived enemy of Iran and the Arab and Islamic world were the European imperialists particularly the British. It should be noted that in the aftermath of World War I, Britain and France had grabbed Arab colonies out of the post-war conquered portions of the Ottoman Empire. The Sykes-Picot Agreement divided much of the Middle East between the two European powers, Britain and France, granting Syria and Lebanon to France and Palestine, or Southern Syria, and Iraq to Britain. In the late 19th Century, Britain had become the "protector" of Egypt and the Sudan and the "defender" of Saudi Arabia. France colonized Algeria in 1830 and expanded its mandate of "protection" in subsequent decades to Morocco and Tunisia. Italy seized Libya from a weakened Ottoman Empire under the rule of the Young Turks in 1911, Britain, France, and Italy controlled the Islamic Horn of Africa, Britain controlled South Yemen and large Islamic populations in India, and Holland controlled the Islamic island archipelago of Indonesia.

Resa Shah admired the State Socialism of Nazi Germany, the Nazis organized and centralized industrialization and control over the culture, and he apparently admired Nazi German crackpot notions that held "Aryans" as a superior race, a concept that gained support specifically in Iran which bought into the mythic notions of its own Aryan racial profile. There is no evidence, however, that Iran embraced Nazi anti-Semitism as the Iranians helped Jews escape from Nazi occupied Europe. Iran helped Jews escape anti-Semitic Iraq after the war, Jews who were trying to make their way to Israel. Until 1978, Iran maintained cordial relations with Israel. After Hitler double-crossed his Soviet Communist allies in June, 1941, by invading Russia in Operation Barbarossa, both Britain and Russia responded by invading Iran in a joint bloodless venture claiming that Resa Shah had tilted to close to the Axis Powers. Resa Shah abdicated and was replaced by his son, the more pro-British Mohammad Resa Pahlavi on September 16, 1941.

The same excuse for interference in the internal affairs of Iran by an imperial power was again used by the British in their 1953 intrigue to depose elected Iranian Prime Minister Mohammad Mossadegh the head of the National Front of Iran, a nationalist party. Responding to decades of British monopoly control over Iranian oil, and after ongoing attempts to negotiate a reasonable equity share of oil revenues with the British failed, Mossadegh nationalized the Anglo-Iranian Oil Company while leaving in place a 25% share to go to settling British claims. The British responded by Winston Churchill falsely claiming to the incoming President Dwight D. Eisenhower that Mossadegh, who was not a Communist but who was rather a left-leaning Iranian nationalist, was a Communist and was a tool of the Soviets. The American administration agreed to help the British overthrow Mossadegh. Either Eisenhower did not want to take any chances at the height of the Cold War with an oil-rich land on the Soviet border or this action was a mistake and one of the few examples where the United States was suckered into supporting

European imperial interests. Either way, the consequences of this aberrational policy has been negative for the United States ever since.

Modern Communism made its presence known in Iran in the latter part of the 19th Century as it attracted the usual suspects, ivory tower intellectuals, academics and the very rich. Secret Communist societies began to sprout in the northern part of the country close to Russia and Azerbaijan. After the 1917 Bolshevik coup in Russia, the 1920 Congress of Eastern Peoples in Baku, the takeover of Gilan Province by the Communist infiltrated Jagual movement followed by the collapse of that Red Army backed state in a wave of blood and misery the following year, the party was banned in Iran and went underground. Strikes and disturbances in 1929-1930 were attributed to underground Communists, strikes and disturbances followed by hundreds of arrests

The Soviet proxy Tudeh Communist Party was founded September 29, 1941, after the British-Russian invasion drove Resa Shah into exile in South Africa. The Tudeh Party reached its peak of popularity in the mid to late 1940's. Roy Mottahedeh, Director of the Harvard Center of Middle Eastern Studies, writing in *The Mantle of the Prophet: Religion and Politics in Iran*, noted that few Iranian intellectuals in those years "dared oppose the party even if they did not join." Respected writer Jalal Al-e-Ahmad resigned from the Tudeh Party complaining of its "nakedly pro-Soviet policies" in 1948. Exposing their dis-loyalty and diminishing their standing with most Iranians, the Tudeh Party demanded that the Iranian government grant special oil rights for the Soviets in the service of "socialist solidarity, internationalism and anti-imperialism" according to Baruch College Professor Ervand Abrahamian, a historian specializing in Iranian history.

Mohammad Mossadegh cracked down on the Tudeh Party and, after the CIA backed coup, Shah Mohammad Reza Pahlevi, a reluctant supporter of the coup, assumed dictatorial powers and continued the crackdown by setting up the increasingly brutal police organization SAVAK. Shah Pahlevi responded to successive crisis, an attempted assassination in 1949, the Mossadegh coup, and other provocations by further concentrating power into his hands. The decades of the 1950's, 60's, and 70's were a time of active and violent rebellion on the part of various Communist and Islamic forces against the strongman government of Reza Pahlevi who, nevertheless, instituted much modernization and reform into his country. There are similarities between Resa Pahlevi and Turkish leader Mustapha Kemal Ataturk except for the fact that Pahlevi was affected by the royal aspect of his dictatorship and that Pahlevi raised the level of violence in his country in response to provocations from Communist forces.

The Soviet backed Tudeh Party emerged as a powerful force in the years leading up to the 1979 overthrow of Resa Pahlevi. Starting in 1977, the Soviet propaganda against the Pahlevi regime, and the internal subversion, was ratcheted up both internally, within Iran, and internationally with a chorus of coordinated propaganda attacks from Communist and pro-Communist groups and assets. The tipping point, however, against Iran and in favor of the replacement of the Pahlevi regime with the Islamo-Communists, was the undermining of that regime by the new American President Jimmy Carter. Regarding Carter, a Senior Iranian diplomat stationed in Washington presciently observed: President Carter betrayed the Shah and helped create the vacuum that will soon be filled by Soviet trained agents and religious fanatics who hate America."

Carter, the champion of "human rights" blackmailed Pahlevi with threats to withhold military aid unless he agreed to major internal reforms. If Carter actually cared about human rights he would have quietly worked with Pahlevi, a staunch American ally since World War II, to improve his human rights policies instead of publically trying to destabilize him and his regime in a manner that dovetailed with the interests of the Soviets. Carter demanded that Pahlevi release "political prisoners," men who were avowed enemies of the state who were involved in conspiracies to overthrow the government, many of whom were terrorists. Carter wanted these prisoners tried in civil courts, as opposed to military tribunals, where they could gain maximum propaganda benefits during their trials. Carter demanded the right to "free assembly" in Iran which allowed

Communists to come out in the open and agitate against the government.

The fashionable Shah Mohammad Resa Pahlevi and his elegant wife Farah Diba visited the White House in November, 1977, a visit that was met with demands from Carter inside the White House while 4 thousand ugly protesters were allowed to mass outside wearing masks, waving clubs, and holding banners for radical communist groups. While the Shah buckled under the pressure from Carter, the Soviets were pouring resources into Iran. The result was an increased level of unrest and terror that accompanied the ominous protests that were launched in major Iranian cities. The Shah was experiencing the scissor effect as he was being undercut from above and below at the same time.

The student protesters, joined by Shiite groups, were mainly well-meaning constitutionalists reminiscent of the constitutional movement of the early 20th Century. They were, however, manipulated by Communist cells financed by and taking their marching orders from the Kremlin. Moscow cynically exploited genuine resentments against the British and, since to overthrow of Mossedegh, America on the part of the Iranians going back over a century. There were confusing rumors on the Iranian street that the CIA, operating under directives from Carter, possibly played a role in the unrest as well, a role reminiscent of that played by the CIA in the overthrow of Mossedegh.

In April, 1978, responding to Carters weakness and worldwide retreat in the face of Communist advances, the Soviets launched a bloody coup in Afghanistan where they installed their puppet Nur Mohammad Taraki who immediately called for "jihad" against his anti-Communist opponents in Afghanistan and Iran. Soviet trained agents and subversives immediately swarmed from Communist Afghanistan into neighboring Iran in what could be described as a full-scale invasion. Training camps were set up and subversives began taking over Shiite Mosques. On January 16, 1979, Shah Resa Palevi fled Iran for exile in the face of over 3 million protesters and a nationwide strike that had been called by Ayatollah Khomeini.

The Ayatollah Ruhollah Khomeni, the exiled Iranian cleric who seized power in Tehran on February 11, 1979, was at least a tool of Communism and very likely himself a Communist dressed in clerical garb. Certainly Khomeini drew support from the Soviet Union and from leftist individuals and groups from around the world both in his takeover and during his ten years in power. Starting in the 1960's, the politically minded Ayatollah began, with his public utterances, to tap into the resentments Iranians have felt toward foreign meddling, tying that resentments to the Shah and throwing Israel into the conspiratorial mix. Khomeini always spoke and wrote in a style that was unmistakably Marxist. Poised to return from exile, Khomeini spoke of establishing a revolutionary Islamic republic, one that would be anti-Western, a euphemism for anti-Capitalist, Socialist, a euphemism for Communist in this case, and one where all power would reside in the hands of the Mullahs. This rhetoric fell on sympathetic ears inside Iran as well-meaning Iranians had been outraged by the increase of the police power of the Shah and his secret police, SAVAK. Khomeni, whose brother had been imprisoned due to his Communist activities in Iran, was calling for a Communist dictatorship, a call that was misunderstood by most Iranians who at first looked to him as a deliverer of greater freedoms. From the time that Khomeini assumed power until today, The Soviet Union, and now Russia, has been and remains the chief sponsor of the revolutionary Mullah regime.

Nureddin Klanuri, head of the Iranian Communist Tudeh Party, in exile in Communist East Berlin, commented regarding Khomeini: *The Tudeh Party approves Ayatollah Khomeini's initiative in creating the Islamic Revolutionary Council. The ayatollah's program coincides with that of the Tudeh Party.* Sadegh Ghothzadeh, Khomeini's handler and closest advisor, was a well-known agent of the Soviet KGB. In January 1978, Pravda, the official Soviet organ, was the first major periodical to officially endorse the Khomeini revolution a year before the takeover.

Left-wing American leaders rallied to the Khomeini banner in 1979 including former Johnson Administration Attorney General Ramsey Clark who held a press conference where he boasted about his trip to Iran and his Paris visit with Khomeini. Clark urged President Carter to take no action to help Pahlevi so that Iran "could determine its own fate." Clark urged Congress to stay out of the crisis. Clark must have observed that no urging was needed on his part regarding Carter. UN Ambassador Andrew Young expressed the left's attitude best when he stated that, if successful, Khomeini would "eventually be hailed as a saint."

Amir Taheri is an Iranian author who has been accused of bias in favor of Pahlevi. Taheri was a trustee of the scholarly Iranian Institute for International Political and Economic Studies in Tehran from 1973 to 1979. He authored *Holy Terror: Inside the World of Islamic Terrorism* in 1987. His work should be understood in the context of his political career and orientation. Taheri reported that it was Heydar Aliyev. post-Soviet President of the Republic of Azerbaijan and at the time a KGB chief, who convinced the Soviets to support Khomeini. Subsequently, according to Taheri, the Communist Tudeh Party was instructed by their Soviet bosses to support Khomeini. The chief secretary of Tudeh, who dissented from the Soviet directive, was replaced by a relative of Khomeini according to Vladimir Kuzichkin, who served as a KGB handler in Tehran and who defected in the 1980's. Kuzichkin also claims that Sadegh Ghotbzadeh, a Khomeini confidant who was executed for allegedly plotting his assassination in September, 1982, was an agent of the Soviet GRU.

Mustafa Ali Chamran who founded a Communist Shi'ite secret society, was a close associate of Ayatollah Khomeini. Chamran, an Iranian scientist, served as the first Defense Minister in Khomeini's Red Mullah Regime and as a personal aide to Khomeini. The revolutionary Chamran also helped found the secretive Amal movement in southern Lebanon by recruiting and training guerilla fighters. Amal was a precursor to the Communist Iranian controlled Hezbollah. Chamran's followers included Iranian foreign minister Ibrahim Yazdi, oil minister Mohammed Gharazi, and Hussein Shaikh al-Islam who led the US Embassy seizure and occupation. Khomeini's close companion, Mohammed Beheshti, who would head the revolutionary government's judicial system, had resided in

East Germany before 1979. Beheshti would die in a mysterious June 28, 1981 bomb explosion.

The Mujahedin e-Khalq was founded September 5, 1965 by Marxist Tehran University students. Seeking to replace the Shah with a Communist government, they considered themselves as Muslims. More radical and anti-American than earlier Iranian Communist groups, they saw no contradiction between Islam and Communism. They engaged in guerilla warfare against the regime of Shah Pahlevi and were behind an unsuccessful airplane hijacking and acts of sabotage that were planned to coincide with the over the top August 1971 2,500 year anniversary celebration of the Iranian Monarchy. The MEK, trained by the Soviet KGB according to journalist Ken Timmerman, fractured into two camps in 1975, one Muslim and one Communist. Both groups participated in the Iranian Revolution but were later apparently purged by Khomeini. They subsequently engaged in guerilla campaigns against the Islamic Republic eventually making their headquarters in Iraq under the sponsorship and with the financial support of Saddam Hussein. In 2012, journalist Seymour Hersh reported that MEK members had contributed to the gathering of Intelligence on the Iranian regime and that some of its members had participated in training in Nevada.

There is some speculation that Grand Ayatollah Ali Khamenei, President of the Islamic Republic 1981-1989 and presently the Supreme Leader of Iran attended Patrice Lumumba University in Moscow. Iranian bloggers discovered a report from Russia Today, February 5, 2010, on the 50th anniversary of the university in which Khamenei is listed a one of its "most notable graduates." The Russia Today's website makes reference to "Iran's Supreme Leader Ali Khomeini," which would be a mis-spelling. Iranian bloggers have identified other Russian sources making the very same claim including the November 25, 2003 issue of Kommersant which presents Khamenei as a "Peoples Friendship University" graduate. This is, of course, sheer speculation.

The November 4, 1979 seizure of the American Embassy by radicals and the holding of 52 American hostages for 444 days, until January 20, 1981, was to the radical Mullah government what the Reichstag fire was to Hitler and the Nazis. The stoking of anti-American frenzy allowed the Mullahs to consolidate their power under a perceived threat of an emergency as they pulled the tail of the United States, the most powerful nation in the world. For the next 10 years, and after a bloody 8 year war with Iraq, the Mullah regime further consolidated its power to the degree that today, Iran is one of the world's most oppressive Communist states in the world, perhaps reviled only in this regard by North Korea.

Iran, in true Communist fashion, views itself as the vanguard of world revolution, both regionally against Iraq where it makes inroads, in Syria where it maintains proxy control over the faltering Syrian regime of the Ba'ath Socialist Bashar al-Assad, and against Israel where it maintains the proxy army Hezbollah in Lebanon, another virtual satellite. Iran remains at war today against Israel, the little Satan, Europe, the mid-sized Satan, and the United States, the Great Satan. Today, Iranian President Mahmoud Ahmadinajad, the totalitarian dictator of Iran, is developing nuclear weapons as quickly as possible as he prepares for the final utopian apocalypse required to usher in the new collectivist age of enlightenment and world peace.

The Islamo-Communist enemies of Israel

- *Children of Israel, remember the blessing I have bestowed upon you, and that I [the Almighty] have exalted you above the nations. [Qur'an - Chapter 2, verse 47]*

- *Bear in mind the words of Moses to his people. He said, 'Remember, my people, the favor which [the Almighty] has bestowed upon you. He has raised up prophets among you, made you kings, and given you that which He has given no other nation. Enter, my people, the holy land which [the Almighty] has given you. Do not turn back, or you shall be ruined.' [Qur'an - Chapter 5, verse 21]*
- *[The Almighty] said to the Israelites, 'Dwell in this land. When the promise of the hereafter comes to be fulfilled, We shall assemble you all together.' [Qu-ran - Chapter 17, verse 104]*

Jewish sovereignty in Judaea suffered a major setback after the Jewish Wars 67-70 CE which resulted in the destruction of the Second Temple by the Roman General Titus. Bar Kochba revolted against Roman rule and achieved Jewish sovereignty for 2 years, 132-136 CE, until his defeat by Hadrian who re-named Judaea "Palestina" after the Philistines, the ancient enemies of the Israelites. The Jews again revolted against the Christian Eastern Roman Empire in 351-352 CE. In 438 CE, Byzantine Empress Eudocia lifted the ban on Jewish prayer in Jerusalem. In 614 CE, the Jews sided with Persia in their war with the Byzantines and established autonomy for 5 years under Persia which were defeated by the re-conquering Byzantines in 625 CE.

Muslim Arab armies defeated the Roman Byzantines 10 years later. The Byzantines surrendered their last garrison at Akko to Umar ibn Al-Khattab, the third Caliph of the Rashidun Caliphate in 637 CE. The Jews of Palestine welcomed the invading Arabs with open arms and Caliph Umar allowed the Jews to once again settle and pray in Jerusalem. Islamic tracts record that Umar helped cleanse the Temple Mount of the filth left by the vengeful Byzantines. Caliph Umar, one of the great rulers of history, was a jurist who established an enduring system of Islamic law. Umar conquered Persia and ruled over an empire that included Arabia, Persia, Palestine, Syria, Egypt, and Libya.

According to 7th Century Armenian Bishop and historian Sebeos, Umar ordered Jews and Muslims to pray together at the site that would become the al-Aqsa Mosque. Umar, according to Sebeos, built the Dome of the Rock for Christians as a shrine that included inscriptions instructing them to not exceed the authority of their faith. The Dome of the Rock was not a Mosque as it has no qibla. Umar encouraged the convening of a Jewish Sanhedrin in Jerusalem by inviting 70 Jewish scholars and their families to settle on the southern end of the Temple Mount.

This author speculates that Umar, who had access to the Book of Kings, a part of the Jewish cannon known as the Tenach and known to Christians as the Old Testament, may have been aware of the fact that Solomon's Temple in Jerusalem was built as a joint project of the Israelites and the Phoenicians as represented by Solomon and the Phoenician King Hiram of Tyre. Perhaps Umar, a religious man and a confidant of the Prophet Mohammad, sought to set the stage for the re-building of the Temple, by both Jews and Arabs, as the precursor to the coming of the Messiah. After 20 years of harmony, the situation began to gradually decline for the Jews of Palestine as, after the assassination of Umar in 644, while on his Hajj in Mecca, the Islamic Caliphate became fractured into warring camps that eventually evolved into the Sunni-Shia schism that continues today.

By the time of the first Crusade, 1095, there was estimated to be over 100 thousand Jews in Palestine. According to many reports the Christian Crusaders slaughtered tens of thousands of Jews and Muslims as they entered Jerusalem and other cities in Palestine, Lebanon and Syria. The Jews of Palestine were devastated by the Crusades and suffered another deadly blow, as did millions of Muslims, as a result of the Mongol Hoards of the 13th and 14th Centuries. Had the Jews not been slaughtered by the Crusades, it is not unreasonable to assume that the Jews would have achieved sovereignty in their homeland in the 11th or 12th Century. The Mongols permanently ended Arab control over much of Palestine as, after the Mongols disappeared, Palestine became a desolate and forgotten portion of the Ottoman Turkish province of Syria for the next 5 Centuries.

In "The Nazi Connection to Islamic Terrorism" published by WND Books, this author wrote about the career of Haj Amin al-Husseini, the British appointed Mufti of Jerusalem, 1922, and how in 1920 he instigated a riot against the Jews of Palestine, the year the British established the Palestine Mandate in land previously part of the Ottoman Turkish province of Syria. Al-Husseini, who was rejected by the Arabs of Palestine in his bid for the position of Mufti because he was viewed by them as not religiously qualified, was nevertheless installed into the position by the British Governor General Sir Herbert Samuel. These policies were the classic British politics of divide and conquer which was the method that the British maintained hegemony at minimum cost. The result was devastating in the British colonies especially in the divisions the British encouraged between Muslims and Hindus in India.

Faisal ibn Hussein al-Hashimi, son of Hussein bin Ali, Sharif of Mecca, claimant of decent from the Prophet Mohammad, King first of Syria and then of Iraq was an enlightened Arab Islamic leader in the true sense of the word. Faisal led the Great Arab Revolt, during World War I, against the Ottoman Young Turk government allied with Imperial Germany. Working with British forces and with assistance from Lawrence of Arabia, Faisal was victorious in the June 1917 Battle of Aqaba which led to the withdrawal of Ottoman forces from Arabia. This victory allowed British General Edmond Allenby to advance from British occupied Egypt into Palestine while Faisal moved on to Damascus which he occupied September, 1918. On October 30, 1918, the Ottomans signed the armistice of Mudros.

British diplomat Henry McMahon had deceitfully promised Hussein bin Ali, Sharif of Mecca, father of Faisal, that the British would recognize a united Arab state if Hussein entered the war against the Turks. Faisal established an Arab government in Syria and in May, 1919, held elections for the establishment of a Syrian National Congress which convened in July. Faisal was proclaimed as King by the Syrian National Congress, March 7, 1920. One month later France invaded Syria from its stronghold in Lebanon after the British handed Syria over to them as a result of the San Remo Conference and in accord with the previously secret 1916 Sykes-Picot line. In what is known as the Franco-Syrian war, Faisal's Syrian forces were defeated in the battle of Maysalun Pass, July 24, 1920, and Faisal fled the country.

General Yusuf al-Azma, the defending Syrian general at Maysalun, was killed in battle. Today Al-Azma is rightfully regarded as a Syrian martyr who died in the cause of Arab independence. The conquering French general Henri Gouraud is reputed have stomped on the grave of the great Arab ruler Saladin and declaring: *The Crusades have ended now! Awake Saladin, we have returned! My presence here consecrates the victory of the Cross over the Crescent.* Faisal, after having fled Syria, become King of Iraq in August, 1921, under British Mandate protection. Faisal's brother Abdullah became Emir of Trans-Jordan the same year, also under British Mandate protection. Trans-Jordan was severed from cis-Jordan by a British commission headed by Winston Churchill, a division that established the Jordan River as the border between the two portions of what had been British Mandate Palestine.

The betrayal of the Arabs by the British and the French after World War I, combined with legitimate grievances that resulted from well over a century of European colonial intrigues and occupations across the Arab and Islamic world starting with Napoleon's conquest of Egypt in 1798, created an atmosphere of distrust of the west that continues to rage in the Islamic world to this day. Indeed, the idea of a conspiracy by foreign powers to control Arab and Islamic lands, secretly or otherwise, has become a staple of the Muslim psyche, accepted as fact by the vast majority of Muslims. Historically, Muslims were absolutely correct to assume that there were conspiracies by Europeans to control their lands. The conquest of Syria, and the humiliation that was heaped upon the nascent Syrian nation by France was a major event in Arab-West relations and the effect of that bold-faced French aggression continues to reverberate. The conspirational view however, while often based upon fact, has also at times been inaccurate and the mindset has at times clouded the judgment and the discernment of Arabs and Muslims leaving them vulnerable to genuine and often home-grown conspiracies. It is argued here that this was the case with the erroneous conspirational view taken by Arabs and Muslims toward the development of Jewish Palestine.

Faisal represented an enlightened view regarding Jewish Palestine, the same genuinely enlightened and fair-minded view he held toward the future of his own Arab people. Faisal's view was held my many if not most Arabs at the end of the war with the potential liberation of vast and oil-rich Arab lands. Faisal and much of the Arab world looked forward to the emergence of Arab sovereign nations to co-exist alongside a small sovereign Jewish state situated in the ancient land of the Jews, land recognized as such by the Koran and by Islamic tradition. Due to conspiratorial thought, however, Faisal's view, and Faisal himself would be undone and his view would become manipulated and replaced by a true conspirator, Haj Amin al-Husseini, the Mufti of Jerusalem. Faisal would become tainted in the eyes of the Arabs for having accepted the position of King in Iraq in 1921 under British sponsorship. He would be viewed as a puppet of a foreign power, Britain, and this view was not entirely without justification.

During the height of Emir Faisal's influence, however, at a time when he was the successful military leader of the Arab revolt, the liberator of Arabia and Syria, the de facto head of state in Syria, the undisputed leader of the Arab nation and, as a recognized decedent of the Prophet Mohammad, the head of Islam, Faisal went to Paris as head of the Arab delegation to the Paris Peace Conference which drew up the terms that ended World War I. The Paris Peace Conference, attended by American President Woodrow Wilson, established the League of Nations. While attending the Conference, Faisal signed an agreement in London, January 3, 1919, with Chaim Weizmann who headed the Zionist delegation to the Paris Peace Conference. It should be noted that the Faisal-Weizmann Agreement, as it is known, was signed by Faisal before France invaded his country in 1920, before the European betrayal of the Arabs was fully revealed.

The Faisal-Weizmann Agreement constituted Arab recognition of Palestine which was the name used at the time to describe the Jewish State. Faisal was the de-facto head of state in Syria at the time he signed the treaty, before the establishment of the British Mandate. As such, Faisal technically controlled what would become Palestine but what was still at the time part of Syria. Therefore, it could be argued that by signing the Faisal Weizmann agreement, Faisal ceded the area to be called Palestine to the Jews. When Palestine declared its independence in 1948, the declaration included the new name of *Israel*. The name change, the establishment of a new name upon independence, one that was closer to the traditions and aspirations of the newly sovereign country, was done in a similar fashion to Persia changing its name to Iran, Ceylon becoming Shri Lanka, Burma becoming Myanmar, Rhodesia becoming Zimbabwe, or British Guinea becoming Guyana. The Faisal Weizmann agreement, legally recognized as part of the Paris Peace agreements and the League of Nations and the Paris Peace Conference, was an expression of the will of the Arabs at the time.

Faisal's father, Hussein Sherif of Mecca, the King of Hijaz had previously set the stage for the agreement by expressing the generally prevailing Arab view in an article that was published in Al Qibla, a Mecca daily newspaper. Hussein stated that Palestine was:

a sacred and beloved homeland of its original sons, the Jews...the return of these exiles to their homeland will prove materially and spiritually an experimental school for their [Arab] brethren.

Hussein called on the Palestinian Arabs to welcome the returning Jews as brethren and he asked the Jews to cooperate with the Arabs for the common welfare. Clearly Sherif Hussein believed that the sovereign Jewish State would benefit the sovereign Arab nation in an experiment in both faith and modernity.

In a December 1918 interview with the London Times, a month before he signed the agreement with Chaim Weizmann in London, Faisal stated in an interview:

The two main branches of the Semitic family, Arabs and Jews, understand one another, and I hope that as a result of interchange of ideas at the Peace Conference, which will be guided by ideals of self-determination and nationality, each nation will make definite progress towards the realization of its aspirations. Arabs are not jealous of Zionist Jews, and intend to give them fair play and the Zionist Jews have assured the Nationalist Arabs of their intention to see that they too have fair play in their respective areas. Turkish intrigue in Palestine has raised jealousy between the Jewish colonists and the local peasants, but the mutual understanding of the aims of Arabs and Jews will at once clear away the last trace of this former bitterness, which, indeed, had already practically disappeared before the war by the work of the Arab Secret Revolutionary Committee, which in Syria and elsewhere laid the foundation of the Arab military successes of the past two years.

After signing the agreement, Faisal wrote letter to Harvard Professor Felix Frankfurter:

The Arabs, especially the educated among us, look with the deepest sympathy on the Zionist movement. Our deputation here in Paris is fully acquainted with the proposals submitted yesterday by the Zionist Organization to the Peace Conference, and we regard them as moderate and proper.

The text of the Faisal Weizmann Agreement is as follows:

3 January 1919

His Royal Highness the Emir Feisal, representing and acting on behalf of the Arab Kingdom of Hedjaz, and Dr. Chaim Weizmann, representing and acting on behalf of the Zionist Organization, mindful of the racial kinship and ancient bonds existing between the Arabs and the Jewish people, and realizing that the surest means of working out the consummation of their natural aspirations is through the closest possible collaboration in the development of the Arab State and Palestine, and being desirous further of confirming the good understanding which exists between them, have agreed upon the following:

Articles:

- *Article I*

The Arab State and Palestine in all their relations and undertakings shall be controlled by the most cordial goodwill and understanding,

and to this end Arab and Jewish duly accredited agents shall be
established and maintained in the respective territories.

- *Article II*

*Immediately following the completion of the deliberations of the
Peace Conference, the definite boundaries between the Arab State
and Palestine shall be determined by a Commission to be agreed
upon by the parties hereto.*

- *Article III*

*In the establishment of the Constitution and Administration of
Palestine, all such measures shall be adopted as will afford the
fullest guarantees for carrying into effect the British Government's
Declaration of the 2nd of November, 1917.(the Balfour Declaration)*

- *Article IV*

*All necessary measures shall be taken to encourage and stimulate
immigration of Jews into Palestine on a large scale, and as quickly
as possible to settle Jewish immigrants upon the land through closer
settlement and intensive cultivation of the soil. In taking such
measures the Arab peasant and tenant farmers shall be protected in
their rights and shall be assisted in forwarding their economic
development.*

- *Article V*

*No regulation or law shall be made prohibiting or interfering in any
way with the free exercise of religion; and further, the free exercise
and enjoyment of religious profession and worship, without
discrimination or preference, shall forever be allowed. No religious
test shall ever be required for the exercise of civil or political rights.*

- *Article VI*

*The Mohammedan Holy Places shall be under Mohammedan
control.*

- *Article VII*

The Zionist Organization proposes to send to Palestine a Commission of experts to make a survey of the economic possibilities of the country, and to report upon the best means for its development. The Zionist Organization will place the aforementioned Commission at the disposal of the Arab State for the purpose of a survey of the economic possibilities of the Arab State and to report upon the best means for its development. The Zionist Organization will use its best efforts to assist the Arab State in providing the means for developing the natural resources and economic possibilities thereof.

- *Article VIII*

The parties hereto agree to act in complete accord and harmony on all matters embraced herein before the Peace Congress.

- *Article IX*

Any matters of dispute which may arise between the contracting parties hall be referred to the British Government for arbitration.

Given under our hand at London, England, the third day of January, one thousand nine hundred and nineteen

Chaim Weizmann, Feisal Ibn-Hussein

Faisal added the following addendum:

Provided the Arabs obtain their independence as demanded in my [forthcoming] Memorandum dated the 4th of January, 1919, to the Foreign Office of the Government of Great Britain, I shall concur in the above articles. But if the slightest modification or departure were to be made [regarding our demands], I shall not be then bound by a single word of the present Agreement which shall be deemed void and of no account or validity, and I shall not be answerable in any way whatsoever.

Faisal thus demanded complete sovereignty for the Arabs in exchange for recognizing the sovereignty of Palestine. Clearly Faisal viewed the establishment of the Jewish State as an organic development of brethren peoples taking their rightful place alongside the Arab nation and he understood such a development to be entirely consistent with Islam. Indeed, Faisal welcomed the emergence of a modern Palestine, a state that would introduce democracy, modern technologies, and economy into the Arab world. Faisal viewed both the fully sovereign Arab States and Palestine developing together in relative political and economic harmony and mutual assistance.

And it was at this point that the misunderstanding entered the picture, a misunderstanding that would be magnified by the appointment of Haj Amin al-Husseini as Mufti of Jerusalem by the British in 1921. Al-Husseini wrongfully labeled the Zionist movement as a European colonialist conspiracy, a view that has remained as a lynchpin for the ongoing Arab war against Israel. It is true, and it should be noted, that the Zionist leader Chaim Weizmann, a British citizen, sought out the assistance of the British to recognize a Jewish State in Palestine after World War I. It is also true that British Foreign Secretary Lord Arthur Balfour issued a letter of intent, the famous 1917 Balfour Declaration, expressing British recognition of the Jewish national home in Palestine after the war. It is also true that the British, falsely as it turned out, promised the Sherif of Mecca British recognition of the Arab nation at the same time.

The Zionist movement, however, constituted an organic and natural immigration of Jews, both European and Arab Jews, to Palestine for the purpose of establishing sovereignty in accord with their political and religious beliefs and rights. The only period in history where there were virtually no Jews in Palestine was during the time of the Christian Crusades. The 19th Century was a time of major Jewish immigration into Palestine, a subsection of the Ottoman province of Syria that was described by visitors, including American writers Mark Twain and Herman Melville as a desolate and virtually empty backwater. The increase in Jewish immigration was accompanied by a concomitant increase in Arab immigration as Arabs sought to benefit economically from the many innovations and the entrepreneurialism of the newly arriving Jews. While there were certainly tensions between the two communities, there was also a great deal of cooperation.

Jewish immigration and the Zionist movement would have continued to grow with or without British recognition and, while history is hindsight, the Zionist enterprise might have been better off without the British who, at any rate, mostly served as obstacles to the movement. Indeed the British, during World War II and while the Holocaust was raging in Europe, diverted valuable resources from the war effort in order to blockade the shore of Palestine in an effort to stop Jewish refugees from making their way onto the shore. The Zionists eventually resorted to arms to drive out the British in 1947, in a manner not unlike the actions taken by the Americans in 1776, but perhaps they would've been better off if they had either gone alone or formed a coalition with the Arabs decades earlier and defeated the British. Perhaps millions of Jews might have found refuge from Hitler.

The Arabs would have benefited from Zionism which, it should be noted, was nothing more and nothing less than the nationalist movement to establish Jewish sovereignty in that small swath of territory between the Jordan River and the Mediterranean Sea. By supporting the modest aspirations of Zionism, the emerging Arab nations would have benefited in their own quest to develop their own political sovereignties and their own cultural and national identities. Faisal and most Arabs in his day intrinsically understood this. It should be noted that it was the Jews of Palestine who, in 1946-1947, finally struck the first blow against the colonialist British and it was the Jews who drove the British out of Palestine. This victory furthered the interests of subsequent successful Arab, Islamic, and third world liberation from European colonialism.

Were the Jews of Palestine Communists? It should be acknowledged that a Marxist and religiously anti-Jewish form of Zionism developed in Europe starting with Moses Hess, the author of Rome and Jerusalem published in 1862. Hess, who was a mentor of Karl Marx, called for a Communist Jewish State in Palestine, one made up of Jews who had renounced their faith, replacing that faith with socialism. It is also true that the followers of Hess achieved the upper hand in the European Zionist movement with their utopian notions but, it should be noted, Theodore Hertzl was not one of them but he was rather a solid Jewish nationalist.

That socialist influence did come to envelop the Zionist establishment in Palestine and while their influence has waned in recent decades, the social Zionists remain as a major and even to a degree a dominant factor within Israel today. The ideology and policies of the social Zionists have held Israel back politically, culturally and economically yet, in spite of their hegemony, Israel has emerged as a vibrant capitalist and freedom oriented nation nevertheless. Regarding Communism in the formal sense, while Stalin aided the Zionists in their war for independence, 1947-1949, and while the Soviet Union was one of the first nations to recognize Israel, the first Israeli Prime Minister David Ben Gurion, who had taken his name from a general in the Bar Kochba rebellion against the Romans, made it clear in 1950 that Israel would look to the United States as its first ally. The history of the influence of the Socialist Zionists on Israel, a topic worth exploring, is beyond the scope of this book. It should be noted, however, that traditional religious Zionism formed a vigorous movement in Russia and Eastern Europe long before Moses Hess and his Communist Zionists and that little known movement also offers a fascinating history that should be studied. The third stream of Zionism, the nationalist movement as represented by the career of American journalist Zev Jabotinsky and the Irgun movement in Israel is also a movement worthy of study.

Was the change in position on the part of the Arabs toward the Jews of Palestine, the change from the views of Faisal to the views of Mufti Husseini, due to Communist influence? Have the subsequent wars against Israel been conducted by Communists or those who have embraced Communist ideas? Obviously anti-Semitism played a role in the war against Israel but mere anti-Semitism is an inadequate explanation. This question must be viewed in the context of the Arab acceptance of the conspiracy theory of the Jews of Palestine as colonial occupiers who should be viewed as comparable to the European conquerors that had picked apart the Arab and Islamic world for over a century. Indeed this was the Communist party line emanating out of the Kremlin as early as 1920 and it remains the leitmotif of both the radical Islam-Communists and their Communist affiliates worldwide to this day.

This false premise regarding the Jews of Palestine came to be accepted by the Arabs because of the association of Jewish Palestine with Britain and the equating of that association with British occupation elsewhere. On its face the idea of the Jews as representing Britain or nay European colonizing nation is ludicrous as obviously the emigrating European Jew, the majority of whom emigrated from Eastern Europe, wanted nothing more than to get out of Europe. This was particularly true in the 1930's, with the gathering storm of anti-Semitism, and the 1940's, during and in the immediate aftermath of the Holocaust. In Palestine this false idea was furthered by the insidious British policy of *divide and conquer* as a means of keeping subject peoples distracted while the British occupied their countries and exploited their markets. The premise was further advanced by the Nazis who falsely portrayed themselves as liberators to the Arabs. The Nazis disingenuously claimed that Germany had no imperialistic agenda even through Germany had previously held colonies in Africa, colonies that were taken away from them after their defeat in World War I.

The war against Israel occurred in three overlapping stages. First the British phase 1920-1948, second the Nazi phase, 1937-1945, and third the Communist phase, 1920 to the present with this phase becoming particularly prominent after 1945. The British war against the Jews of Palestine was launched when Sir Herbert Samuel, Governor General of the British Mandate of Palestine, appointed Haj Amin al-Husseini as Mufti of Jerusalem in 1921. Al-Husseini had been previously indicted for instigating a bloody slaughter of Jews in Jerusalem in 1920, an incident known in Israel as Bloody Passover.

There was considerable evidence to suggest that the British had incited the 1920 anti-Zionist riots and that incitement likely included anti-Semitic British officers. This was believed to be the case by the Zionist leadership at the time which was why they referred to the riots as a pogrom, the word that had been previously used to describe the planned attacks on Russian Jewish communities that were organized by the Russian Tsar. British Palestine Mandate Governor Sir Herbert Samuel, himself a liberal British Jew, pardoned al-Husseini, invited him back to Jerusalem, and appointed him as Mufti over the objections of the Palestinian Arabs. Mufti Husseini would subsequently head the Arab Higher Committee which meant that he was the de-facto head of Arab Palestine comparable to the role the President of the Palestinian Authority plays today. The objection on the part of the Palestinian Arabs to al-Husseini as Mufti was that he was not sufficiently knowledgeable in Islamic law. This begs the question in terms of whether or not al-Husseini was a genuine Muslim leader or whether he was a political agent of change.

During his 1921-1936 tenure, the Mufti worked with the British authorities to create conflict between Jews and Arabs while developing a terrorist network. In 1936, after the Mufti had been exiled from Palestine due to his role in the Arab Revolt and due to British suspicion that he was on the Nazi payroll after having allegedly met with Adolf Eichmann during Eichmann's brief visit to Haifa, al-Husseini began the tactic of sending in suicide bombers who were directed against Arabs who worked with the British or the Jews. Such terror tactics have no firm tradition in Islamic culture which raises the question of whether the method was inspired by the Communists.

The August 24th 1929 Hebron Massacre, instigated by the Mufti, also had the earmarks of a Communist inspired event. Indeed the previous Jaffa riots of May 1-7, 1921, were launched by the Jewish Communist Party on May Day with the intent of overthrowing the British Mandate government and establishing a Soviet Palestine. Fights between different left-wing groups of parading Communist factions in Tel Aviv spilled over into Arab Jaffa. The 1929 massacre of the ancient and indigenous Jews of Hebron went well beyond the conventional rules of war as observed by Muslims for centuries. Traditional Islam generally spared women and children and this was not the case in Hebron. Indeed heroic local Arabs shielded and protected their Jewish neighbors from militant gangs who showed up as if out of nowhere. Many left-wing Jews in Palestine, perhaps reflecting on the Jaffa disturbances, believed that the Hebron massacre was inspired by Stalin and they disavowed Communism as a result. After the Hebron massacre, the Palestine Communist Party released a statement that said in effect that a revolutionary movement without pogroms is impossible. After the massacre of 68 Jews, the British proceeded to ethnically cleanse the Hebron survivors by forcing them to move to Jerusalem. This was the beginning of a British policy of forcibly evicting Jewish communities from the region that is now known as the West Bank.

The warring Communist factions in Jewish Palestine united in 1923 to form the Palestine Communist Party which was admitted to the Communist International and placed under Soviet control in 1924. The price of admission to Soviet control was that the Palestine Communist Party accepted a line from the Kremlin that offers insight into the Soviet agenda in the Arab world then and reflects the left-wing and Communist viewpoint today. The Palestine Communist Party agreed to support Arab sovereignty in Palestine and it stood *opposed to British imperialism and denounced Zionism as a movement of the Jewish bourgeoisie allied to British imperialism.* In line with the policies of the Mufti, the treacherous Palestine Communist Party opposed Jewish immigration and worked underground in a revolutionary effort to recruit Arab members. Given the secretive nature of Communism in general, it is difficult to definitively discern the exact nature of the Communist involvement in the riots and revolts that rocked Palestine from the 1920's until Israel declared its independence in April, 1948. There is little doubt the Palestine Communist Party, controlled from Moscow, coordinated its subversive activities with the Mufti.

The Mufti was the first leader to send a congratulary telegram to Adolf Hitler upon his election as Chancellor of Germany in 1933. Thus began a courtship between the Mufti and the Nazis, a courtship that included the Mufti aiding a pro-Nazi coup in Iraq in 1941 and the Mufti spending the World War II years in Nazi Berlin where he was in charge of a virtual Arab-Nazi Government in Exile. Mufti Husseini met with Hitler who promised him that he would be chief "Arab administrator" in the Middle East once the Germans liberated the region from the British. Hitler referred to the Mufti and the Fuhrer of the Arab world. At the January, 1942 Wansee Conference, the Nazis established their policy of extermination of the Jews of Europe. This conference took place less than two months after the Mufti met with Hitler on November 30, 1941. Before Wansee, the Nazi policy was to expel the Jews. The published notes of that meeting indicate that the Mufti al-Husseini and Hitler discussed "the Jewish problem."

Dieter Wisliceny, who was Adolf Eichmann's lieutenant in the Holocaust stated, in testimony that was introduced at Nuremburg and at the Eichmann trial, that the Mufti called for the murder of the Jews of Europe and that he was *even more important than Adolf Eichmann* in the implementation of the genocide. The Mufti was assigned by Heinrich Himmler to oversee the development of the Muslim Bosnian SS Hanjar Brigades in Croatia and other Muslim units, brigades that fought fiercely on the Russian front and elsewhere. The Mufti played a role in the Holocaust against the Jews of Europe, touring the death camps and sending letters to Nazi puppet leaders in Eastern Europe urging them to send their Jews to "Poland" for re-settlement. The Mufti was a personal friend of Adolf Eichmann and Heinrich Himmler and his finances were handled by Swiss Nazi banker Francois Genoud who also assisted him in the funneling of money, the "sonderfund" money "expropriated" from Jews as they were sent to the gas chambers, into the Middle East, through Genoud's Swiss bank accounts, to finance pro-Nazi cells.

The Mufti returned to Cairo and a hero's welcome after the end of the war, one step ahead of a possible indictment at Nuremburg for war crimes pertaining to the atrocities committed in Yugoslavia by the Hanjar Brigades. The Mufti led efforts in the post-war years to help escaping Nazi war criminals make their way to Arab capitals where many of them assumed Arab names and converted to Islam. In 1946, the Zionists in Palestine were denied information they sought to indict the Mufti by the British. It was reported that soldiers wearing Hanjar uniforms fought Israel in 1947-1949. The Mufti was implicated in the 1948 assassination of King Abdullah of Jordan as Abdullah was about to sign a peace treaty with Israel.

The Mufti was likely neither a Communist nor a Nazi but rather the Mufti worked with any group or nation that assisted him in his goal of eradicating Israel. He established modern terrorism by patenting the suicide bomber which he aimed not at Jews but at moderate

Arabs. Indeed the murder of moderate Arabs and Muslims has remained a hallmark of the Islamo-Communist movement and that tactic has all too often been aided by the well-meaning West. The real losers have been genuine moderate Muslims and the citizens of Muslim nations. The Mufti was responsible for introducing a racist form of Jew hatred into Islamic society, a form that he borrowed whole cloth from the Nazis who he devoutly served. The Mufti played a role in establishing the permanent refugee camps and preventing the willing Arab states from absorbing the refugees as any normal nation would do. In his last public appearance, after his appointment as head the World Islamic Congress in 1962, the Mufti al-Husseini exhorted all Arab and Muslim nations to expel their indigenous Jewish citizens from their lands.

After the 1945 defeat of Nazi Germany, the Soviet Union and the international Communist movement became the primary promoter of Islamic radicalism and the developer of Islamo-Communism. Specifically, the Arab war against Israel and the entire Arab radical movement was usurpt by Islamo-Communism under Soviet influence and in many cases direct involvement. Muhammad Abd al-Rahman ar-Rauf al-Qudwah al-Husaini, better known by his nome de guerre Yasir Arafat, picked up the radical mantle from the Mufti al-Husseini by establishing the Soviet trained terror cell al-Fatah. Arafat was absolutely and unabashedly a Communist. The Soviet Communists, who sponsored Arafat, became the dominant players in terms of promoting Islamic terrorism after the 1945 demise of the Nazis who were previously the main sponsors. Unlike the Iranian Mullah's, Arafat made little pretension toward being a Muslim but rather Arafat reveled in his status as a dedicated Communist revolutionary.

Ion Mihai Pacepa, a two star general in the Romanian Communist Securitate, an intelligence advisor to Romanian Dictator Nicholae Ceausescu, became the highest ranking Communist defector to the west when, July, 1978, he received asylum in the United States, an asylum granted by President Jimmy Carter. Pacepa authored the international bestseller *Red Horizons* which played a direct role in the toppling of the Ceausescu regime. In an article published in the Wall Street Journal, September 22, 2003, *The KGB's Man* Pacepa claimed that Arafat was trained by the Soviet KGB at the Balashikha special operations school located east of Moscow in the mid 1960's.

Regarding Arafat Pacepa wrote:

Before I defected to America from Romania, leaving my post as chief of Romanian intelligence, I was responsible for giving Arafat about $200,000 in laundered cash every month throughout the 1970s. I also sent two cargo planes to Beirut a week, stuffed with uniforms and supplies. Other Soviet bloc states did much the same. Terrorism has been extremely profitable for Arafat. According to Forbes magazine, he is today the sixth wealthiest among the world's "kings, queens & despots," with more than $300 million stashed in Swiss bank accounts.

It should be noted that one of the classic tell-tale signs that a leader of a nation or an organization is a Communist is that they live a life of wealth and luxury that would in many cases make a successful American corporate capitalist blush. This has been true of most Communist leaders from Lenin to Stalin and including Mao, Ho Chi Minh, Fidel Castro, and Kim il Sung. The difference between the Communist leader and the corporate capitalist, besides the usual difference in terms of the vulgar extravagance of the Communist leader versus the generally more modest tastes of the capitalist, is that the Communist lives off the "expropriated" wealth of others. A classic example of this practice was when Communist Daniel Ortega, upon becoming Dictator of Nicaragua, seized the best mansions in Managua, took one for himself and handed the rest out to his friends, family, and political associates. Ortega and his friends were able to hold on to their loot as a condition of his stepping aside in 1989 when he actually ceded power in an act that is rare in the Communist world. Karl Marx actually set the tone for this practice given that he was supported throughout his life by wealthy industrialists and inheritances. There is a sense of entitlement for the Communist in the indulgence in the material pleasures that wealth provides and that is that the Communist leader is, after all, a hero of the masses. Arafat was one of the worst offenders.

Arafat was a master of deception. In the Wall Street Journal article *The KGB's Man* Pacepa wrote that he instructed Arafat while he was secretly in Bucharest March 1978, on strategies for approaching the west. Pacepa wrote that his instructions to Arafat were: *You simply have to keep on pretending that you'll break with terrorism and that you'll recognize Israel -- over, and over, and over.* Pacepa reported that his boss, Ceausescu, was *euphoric over the prospect that both Arafat and he might be able to snag a Nobel Peace Prize with their fake displays of the olive branch.*

One month later Pacepa accompanied Ceausescu on an official trip to Washington where he was feted by President Carter. Ceausescu warned Carter that he must extend every effort to promote peace in the Middle East or suffer *severe consequences.* Privately, according to Pacepa, Ceausescu promised Carter that Arafat would end the terrorism and that the PLO would become a law-abiding government-in-exile if Carter established diplomatic recognition. Carter, the naive westerner, publically hailed the repressive Communist Romanian Dictator as a *great national and international leader* who had *taken on a role of leadership in the entire international community.* Carter approved a joint communique declaring Ceausescu as serving *the cause of the world.*

Declassified Soviet archives indicate that in 1973 Arafat's PLO members traveled to North Vietnam where they met with Communist strategists. The PLO had been amazed and bewildered by how the North Vietnamese Communists were able to generate support from American and international student movements. The PLO, up until that point had simply failed to catch on. The North Vietnamese explained to their PLO fellows that such presentations as calling for the slaughter of all the Jews and for driving the Jews into the sea was not likely to win them any friends among fashionable student and intellectual circles. The North Vietnamese revealed the secret to their success which was their ability to package their invasion of South Vietnam as a "liberation" movement. They suggested that the PLO change their rhetoric from the crude and honest blood-thirsty type to high-minded talk about liberation and oppression by Israel as an imperialist European colonialist power.

Dr. George Habash was the founder of the Marxist-Leninist *Popular Front for the Liberation of Palestine* in 1967. The PFLP, the second largest member of the PLO, second to Arafat's al-Fatah, patented many of the tactics of Arab terror including hijackings which were responsible for the killing of 20 American citizens and the first hostage taking in the late 1960's and early 1970's. According to Soviet intelligence defector Konstantin Preobrazhensky, the PFLP maintained a longtime association with the Soviet KGB. Of Christian background, Habash and his family had fled from his home in the Arab city of Lydda in 1948 as Israeli units advanced during the war of Israeli independence. Habash graduated from the American University in Beirut with a degree in medicine in 1951.

Drawing members from students at American University in Beirut and students from Libya, Saudi Arabia and Kuwait, Habash was one of the founders of the Arab Nationalist Movement in 1953. The Arab Nationalist Movement was a secular left-wing pan-Arab movement that advocated socialism and armed struggle. Respected Middle East journalist John K. Cooley interviewed Habash with comments published in his book *Green March Black September: The Story of the Palestinian Arabs* London, 1973. Cooley wrote that Habash expressed the opinion that the cause of the Arab defeat by Israel in 1948, what he falsely claimed was a conspiracy of *Israel-Britain-US Zionist* interests, to be the: *scientific society of Israel as against our own backwardness in the Arab world. This called for the total rebuilding of Arab society into a twentieth-century society.*

This analysis is partially based on Habash's assumption that the left orientation of Zionism was its source of strength as opposed to the traditional Islamic orientation of the Arabs which he viewed as backward and as a source of weakness. Given his indisputable political orientation, Habash was calling for Arab society to be re-built as Communist as opposed to as a free market society retaining its Islamic orientation. The fact that Habash drew membership for his left-wing organization from college students is not a unique phenomenon. Indeed, all Communist movements have always recruited from amongst College students and Communism has always been a trendy idea with a large swath of College Professors and the intellectuals in general. The backbone of the Nazi movement was made up of the same type of students and intellectuals.

The profile of most of the students who have been and are attracted to Communism is that they are either from privileged and often sheltered backgrounds, that their parents were Communist as has often been the case in the United States, or that they are classic camp followers. The rich adherents and, make no mistake, the wealthiest families in history and today often contain members with communist orientations, seek the excitement of thinking that they can change the world and that they can use their wealth, more often than not unearned, as a vehicle for the indeterminate change. Enjoying the comfort and security that material wealth often provides, Communism offers a sense of going beyond their sheltered environs and "making a difference" in the world by using that wealth to transform human nature. More likely the wealthy Communist is not aware that their program of change would make it more difficult for those with less to improve their lot or even become wealthy themselves. The camp follower just wants to be close t wealth and power, to be one of the so-called beautiful people. The entire endeavor , in spite of vigorous denial, requires a large portion of conformity both in external effects and in the inner mind and inner life. Ironically, such conformity is exactly what Communism is ultimately all about, the negation of the individual in favor of the collective.

Habash told John Cooley that: *We held the 'Guevara view' of the 'revolutionary human being.... A new breed of man had to emerge, among the Arabs as everywhere else. This meant applying everything in human power to the realization of a cause.* Certainly the monotheistic faiths teach their adherents to become better human beings, to be *born again in Christ* in the case of Christianity, and to thus improve their societies through the advocacy of morals and the good life but the improvements are based upon free will, which implies the existence of the individual, and within the context of human fallibility, which is both a spiritual concept and a practical observation of reality. The *'revolutionary human being.... new breed of man* is a fiction which is why force is required to attempt something against human nature. Habash calls for *applying everything in human power to the realization of a cause.* This is a call for an earthly world totalitarian dictatorship, brought about by *everything in human power* at the point of a gun. Only faith and freedom will lead the individual to happiness and society to progress.

The Arab loss of the six day war in June, 1967 resulted in Habash becoming the head of a merger between the Arab Nationalist Movement, Youth for Revenge and the Syrian backed Palestine Liberation Front founded by radical Marxist Ahmed Jebril who later broke away and formed the pro-Syrian PFLP-GC. The radical Marxist Jebril was credited with responsibility for the *Night of the Gliders* over Israel, November 25, 1987 and has been more recently credited with attempts to run the Gaza blockade with arms shipments.

It must be acknowledged that the Palestinian Arabs of Israel have a legitimate claim to Arab independence. It is the contention of this author that, regarding the ongoing civil conflict between Palestinian Jews and Palestinian Arabs, the Jews simply have the stronger case to make. The Arabs have achieved sovereignty in 24 Nations, from the Atlantic to the Persian Gulf. These nations cover a vast area with great cities, creative citizens, and in many cases extraordinary oil resources. The sovereignty of the Arabs, alongside a small Jewish Palestine, was promised to Emir Faisal ibn Hussein as the primary condition for his signing the Faisal-Weizmann agreement in 1919, an agreement in which the Arab leader recognized Jewish Palestine. While the Israelis have a long way to go in terms of rights for their Palestinian Arab minority, the Palestinian Arabs have nevertheless achieved a demonstrable degree of progress in Israel in terms of civil and religious rights. In a poll conducted by the Council on Foreign Relations, released January 2011, only 30% of Jerusalem Arabs said they favored Palestinian Arab citizenship over Israeli citizenship.

Indeed, the Palestinian Arab nation achieved sovereignty when the Kingdom of Jordan became sovereign on May 24, 1946. Ahmad Shukeiri, one of the founders of the PLO declared *Jordan is Palestine and Palestine is Jordan.* In every way the Arabs west of the Jordan and the Arabs east of the Jordan are the same people. This author suggests that for political and religious reasons, the Palestinian Arabs of Israel would be well advised to eschew the destructive and divisive left-wing propaganda that divides them from their Israeli Jewish brethren. They should consider embracing the Jewish destiny of Israel as loyal non-Jewish minorities aiding in the fulfillment of their nation's mission and destiny, one that is entirely consistent with the Koran. Certainly the Palestinian Authority of Israel ought to continue to represent the Arabs of the West Bank and Gaza, and the position of President of the Palestinian Authority ought to be elevated to the position of Vice Prime Minister of Israel.

PLO member Abu Iyad, in his memoir published in Arabic entitled *Palestinian Without A Motherland*, wrote that while he was in North Vietnam as part of the PLO delegation, the North Vietnamese advised the PLO to *stop talking about annihilating Israel and instead turn your terror war into a struggle for human rights. Then you will have the American people eating out of your hand.* Like Arafat, the North Vietnamese dictator Ho Chi Minh, whose real name was Nyugen ai Quoc, was a Soviet agent and, in Ho's case he had been an agent for 20 years before he became a public figure in North Vietnam in 1945. The PLO admired how rapidly the North Vietnamese overran South Vietnam after the US Congress cut off aid to their South Vietnamese allies in March, 1975. Perhaps the PLO hoped that with the right posturing and with the same cultivation of the same friends, the same result might befall Israel.

The North Vietnamese, according to Abu Iyad, recommended a two stage program to destroy Israel. The first stage involved the improved Public Relations and this immediately bore fruit with Arafat invited to address the United Nations General Assembly. He delivered his speech with a gun fastened to his belt. This was followed by the UN voting to approve a slogan equating Zionism with racism. The second stage was the so-called two state solution to the crisis that the Communist Arafat and his co-horts had worked so hard to promote. Once Israel was forced, due to international pressure, to surrender its sovereignty to a large percentage of its tiny territory to what would be a Communist state headed by the PLO, Arafat and his cadres would be in a position to finish Israel off. The

North Vietnamese and the PLO both viewed the new state as nothing more than a vanguard move to destroy Israel in two stages.

On September 13, 1993, Arafat, wearing military fatigues, signed an agreement with Israeli Prime Minister Yitzhak Rabin on the lawn of the White House with American President Bill Clinton presiding. This agreement was supposed to mean that steps would be taken on the part of the Israelis to aid in the establishment of a Palestinian Arab state in the areas known as the West Bank and Gaza. In exchange, Arafat signed a document promising to stop the war and the incitement. On that same day, in a pre-taped interview that ran on Jordan TV, Arafat explained in Arabic: *Since we cannot defeat Israel in war, we do it in stages. We take any and every territory that we can of Palestine and establish sovereignty there, and we use it as a springboard to take more. When the time comes, we can get the Arab nations to join us for the final blow against Israel.*

Arafat was, indeed, a master of deception but his methodology, contrary to the assumptions of many, was not derived from Islam but rather from a radicalized Islamo-Communism. It is true that there are Islamic tracts that grant permission for the Muslim to deceive, to engage in al-taqiyya, but those tracts primarily pertain to situations in which the Muslim might be in personal danger due to his religion. There is also no question that Islamic verses can and have been interpreted to mean that it is ok to deceive. It is also true that Jews, Christians, and indeed every individual alive today or in the past has in one way or another engaged in a conscious deception at one time or another. The monotheistic faiths, at their core, reject deception as they believe that they are founded on the transcendent truth of a creator of the universe who is the giver of revealed moral and ethical laws that are true.

The Communist inspired Muslim terrorists changed the definition of Islamic tracts and then merged those tracts with the fundamental nature of Communism itself which is, in fact, the greatest and oldest deception in history. The Communist is encouraged to lie, to create new truths, new realities to suit a re-invention of man. Ever Communist tract is soaked with lies because Communism itself is the great lie that human beings can be as God knowing everything

God knows. Indeed even a cursory conversation with a Communist, or a person conditioned to think like a Communist, reveals almost a separate language, a separate form of communication. That language is the language of innuendo, double-speak, deception, deliberate vagaries and abstractions, and, when necessary, downright lies. Dear reader. Please take not of how difficult it is to discern exactly what such a person is talking about when they express a political opinion.

The Communist is not only encouraged to lie but lying in the service of Communism is considered a virtue and a fine art. This is the art and science of the dialectic, the ability, in Hegelian fashion, to hold two opposite opinions in virtually the same sentence without the listener being able to detect that this has occurred. It has been said in Communist circlers that Robert Minor, a Communist journalist and one of the founders of the American Communist Party in 1919, was one of the most accomplished dialecticians in his day. Minor was so good at articulating the dialectic, holding opposing views in the same talk, that it would take some time for the most experienced listener to detect that he had been deceived.

The Catechism of a Revolutionary was written by Russian revolutionary Sergey Nechayev in 1869. This manifesto was of central importance in the development of modern Communism and it was widely disseminated and re-published in whole or in part in Communist publications around the world. The *Catechism* describes the true Communist as an amoral man, a soul-less human resource who exists to serve the revolution. Nechayev's Communist is permitted to commit any crime or any deception necessary to effect a Communist victory. Nechayev's Communist is called to engage in any act that would destroy anyone or any institution deemed as an obstacle standing in the way of the ultimate Communist victory.

The opening lines of the *Catechism of a Revolutionary* read as follows:

The revolutionary is a doomed man. He has no private interests, no affairs, sentiments, ties, property nor even a name of his own. His entire being is devoured by one purpose, one thought, one passion - the revolution. Heart and soul, not merely by word but by deed, he has severed every link with the social order and with the entire civilized world; with the laws, good manners, conventions, and morality of that world. He is its merciless enemy and continues to inhabit it with only one purpose - to destroy it. –

Clearly this is the creed of the Islamo-Communist and ethos strangely harkens back to a most pure and primitive principle. By severing his link to the social order, the revolutionary has subsumed his own identity and has, as such, redefined reality in his own mind. The Islamo-Communist has no interest, as such, in advancing the interests of the thousand year old culture and social order of Islam, a social order that is based upon moral and ethical principles. The Islamo-Communist seeks to destroy that culture and social order, to re-invent it, and he has convinced himself that he conducts that re-invention for the good of others.

Like all cultures and nations, Islam has been influenced by other cultures and nations. Regarding western culture, Islam had two choices in terms of which influence it would embrace. Islam could have chosen the fruit of western culture, the one best exemplified by the United States, a culture that is based upon Godly principles and laws, one that respects the natural God given rights of the individual to be free in a social order based on faith and truth. This idea is not exceptional to the United States, not to be viewed in a chauvinistic context as these ideas are available to all peoples and are natural because they are right.

Or Islam could have been influenced by the other fruit of western culture, the one best exemplified by Nazi Socialism and Soviet Communism, both evil fruits exported into the Islamic world from the dark side of the European enlightenment. Those modern western social and political experiments were based upon the principle that Man, not God, was the creator of all rights, which were to be viewed as privileges granted by the man controlled enlightened state. This idea, which goes back to the ancient days of idol worship and the Oriental ancient King as god on earth, is, in fact, the ultimate in chauvinism. This is because, in the outer sense, Communism ultimately represents the physical control of the entire world by a clique of men who hold all power over life and death and, in the inner sense, Communism involves the colonization and slavery of the human mind and the human soul. It is never too late for Muslims, those Muslims who genuinely care about their own faith and future, to look into their own souls and determine not only what is right but what is most authentically Islamic.

The First Book of Kings, Chapter 7, viewed as Holy by all three monotheistic faiths, recounts an event concerning a certain Hiram of Tyre. Born of an Israeli mother, or the tribe of Naphtali, and a Tyrean father, of the nation that would come to be known as Phoenicia, Hiram, as such represented both nations. Hiram was known to King Solomon as a man who knew how to work in brass. Solomon was planning the building of the Temple to the LORD in Jerusalem. Solomon hired Hiram and sent for him. The Book of Kings records, in intricate and beautiful detail, exactly how Hiram, the Israeli-Phoenician, built the foundations of the Temple to the LORD. Solomon himself crafted the various ritual items that were required for religious purposes.

Kings II Chapter 8 recounts how Solomon and the Levites, the priestly sect specifically designated by God in Sinai to serve the Israelites, and by extension all of mankind, in terms of carrying out the functions of worship, brought the Ark of the Covenant into the Holy of Holies. Inside the Ark of the Covenant rested the two stone tablets received by Moses. Thus the Israelites, and their successor peoples, the Jews, the Christians, and the Muslims, did not worship idols, graven images presented by deceitful men who sought power and engaged in a hoax to fool their nations into surrendering their rights and identities. Solomon and the Israelis were respecting and venerating what was essentially a book, two stone pages with instructions written on them. The Israelis respected the law, as revealed by the divine, thus the Israelites rendered respect for basic truths.

Kings II Chapter 9 introduces Hiram, King of Tyre who is not the same Hiram as Hiram the builder. King Hiram of Tyre supplied Solomon with cedar trees, fir trees and gold to build the Temple to the LORD and other buildings. King Hiram of Tyre and King Solomon of Israel engaged in diplomatic relations and trade. Hiram sent skilled workers to assist Solomon in the building of his Navy.

The relevant message to be derived from this Biblical scenario is that the ancient precursors of the Israelis and the Arabs of today, the ancient Israelis and the ancient Phoenicians, worked closely together for a common purpose and that purpose was to build the Temple of the LORD. Perhaps these Holy passages in the Book of Kings, revered by both Jews and Muslims, passages containing both historical and religious significance, contain a message, both practical and spiritual, and they contain a path forward for relations between the two brethren peoples who populate Israel today. May a way be found where the peoples of both nations, Jews and Muslims, find a way to come together and once again form a joint effort to rebuild the House of the LORD. May such an effort, as recorded in the Holy book of old, bring about the coming of the Messiah speedily in our own day.

Amen.

Islam and the Soviet Union

Communism and Arab and Islamic states

Saudi Arabia

Saudi Arabia was established in 1744 when an oath was taken between Muhammad bin Saud, the tribal Emir of the desert town of al-Diriyah, and Muhammad ibn Abd al-Wahhab, the founder of the Sunni Wahhabi sect of Islam. Al-Diriyah is located near the modern Saudi capital city of Riyadh. In the 18th Century, Arabia was made up of loosely allied tribes who were under the suzerainty of the Ottoman Empire. The pact between the political and religious leader was codified by the marriage of the Saudi prince Abdul-Aziz and a daughter of al-Wahab. The alliance continues unbroken and remains in place today.

The Saudi's established control over most of Arabia, including Mecca and Medina, which caused the ire of the Ottoman Sultan who responded by attacking Saudi Arabia, 1811-1818, through their allies Egypt which was under the rule of Muhammad Ali Pasha. The Egyptians destroyed the Saudi capital of al-Diriyah and sent Saudi ruler Abdullah to Istanbul as a prisoner where he was beheaded and where his head was unceremoniously tossed into the Bosporus. The second Saudi state, which established its capital in Riyadh, never captured Mecca and Medina from the Turks and was wracked by instability and family quarrels often resulting in assassinations.

King Abdul-Aziz, known in the west as ibn Saud, raided and seized Riyadh from his rival, the Ottoman sponsored Rashid clan on

January 15, 1902, and established what is known as the third Saudi state. Ibn Saud ruled until his death November 9, 1953. Involved in ongoing internecine conflict with the Ottoman backed Rashid clan he formed an alliance with the British. He drove the Hashemites out of the Hijaz, which included Mecca and Medina in 1925 at that point consolidating control over the area the Saudis presently control. Oil was discovered in 1938 which helped the Saudis to create and maintain one remains as of the world's most centralized and authoritarian regimes. After 1945 America became the chief sponsor of the Saudi's replacing the role played by the British who had lost power after World War II.

Conclusion

Radical Islamists view the secular influence of the West as a threat to Islam and as a source of corruption. They view themselves as enmeshed in an eternal war with those nations and individuals that represent corrupting western ideas. They view the world as divided between two spheres, the world or war, or the Dar es Harb, which is the non-Islamic world including Arab and Islamic nations controlled by governments they consider to be corrupt, and the world of peace, or the Dar es Salaam, which is the portion of the world that is under the control of the Islamists. The Islamists share with secular Communism the belief that a process of Jihad, what the Communists call revolution, is required to fight the corrupt element within their own ranks as well as the means to cleanse humanity and to ultimately subsume the entire planet into a one world government.

Radical Islam and Communism have much in common in terms of beliefs and goals. Islam tends to be materialist when compared to the other two monotheistic faiths as Islam tends to view human experience as primarily an earthly function in the here and now as opposed to an experience that includes a spiritual side and an afterlife. Communism is completely materialistic as Communism strives to erase the past, to exist entirely in the present, and to shape shift reality at will in order to create a new and yet undermined future.

Islam is a political and military as well as a religious and spiritual system and, as such, Islam leaves the door slightly open to Communism which is completely political and military. This is why Communism was able to kick open the Islamic door and why many Radical Islamists un-wittingly were duped into an erroneous understanding of their own faith. Other Islamists were fully witting and conscious participants in an international Communist conspiracy. Most radical Islamists fall somewhere in the middle of those two definitions as many have accepted a radicalized and hybridized version of their faith without being fully conscious of the Communist influence that manufactured and shaped that faith.

Thus the irony, the contradiction between the basic claims on the part of the radical Islamists that they reject the corrupt ways of the west while in fact they are themselves the product of the very corruption that they rail against. The radical Islamist movement has imbibed very deeply at the well of atheistic left-wing Communism and the result has been an utterly corrupted and, in the worst sense, a westernized and hybridized form of Islam. In the process the radical Islamists have sold out their traditions, their moral code, their faith and their own Islamic people.

Islam was corrupted by both Nazi Socialism and by Communism. These two poisonous products of the European enlightenment represent the worst fruits of western secular politics and culture. Islam has been exploited by Nazi and Communist theoreticians, agents, and activists who have taken specific aspects of Islam, those that mirror Communism itself, and then magnified those aspects while shaking off the more traditional as well as the more genuinely progressive aspects. The result has been a new religion, Islamo-Communism, a religion that only contains cosmetic similarities with authentic Islam. Islamo-Communism is at war today with both its own people and with the western world and that war is virtually identical, with cultural differences, to the old war between the west and the Nazis and then the war with the Communists. The old enemies of freedom enslaved millions and today that enemy still holds a large portion of the world under its heel while they continue marching on the free world.

* 9 7 8 1 0 9 3 6 6 8 2 0 9 *